Monique Combes

Photography by Paul Ste

TERRY CLOTH

Schiffer Publishing Ltd

4880 Lower Valley Road • Atglen, PA 19310

Other Schiffer Books on Related Subjects:
Fashion Fabrics: 1960s, 0-7643-0584-0, $29.95
The Synthetic '70s: Fabric of the Decade, 0-7643-0717-7, $24.95

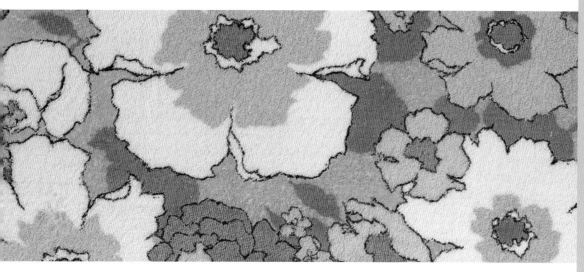

All brand names discussed in the text are registered and trademarked by their owners.

All images are the property of the author unless otherwise noted. My husband has photographed most of the fabrics in Chapter 10, additional images in other chapters, and provided editing skills to images presented from other attributed sources. The items photographed are vintage or antique, and may show some characteristics of age, soiling, and use.

Designed by RoS
Type set in Bernard MT Condensed/Agenda-MediumCondensed

ISBN: 978-0-7643-4185-4
Printed in China

Published by Schiffer Publishing, Ltd.
4880 Lower Valley Road
Atglen, PA 19310
Phone: (610) 593-1777; Fax: (610) 593-2002
E-mail: Info@schifferbooks.com

For the largest selection of fine reference books on this and related subjects, please visit our website at:
www.schifferbooks.com.
You may also write for a free catalog.

This book may be purchased from the publisher.
Please try your bookstore first.

We are always looking for people to write books on new and related subjects. If you have an idea for a book, please contact us at:
proposals@schifferbooks.com.

Schiffer Books are available at special discounts for bulk purchases for sales promotions or premiums. Special editions, including personalized covers, corporate imprints, and excerpts can be created in large quantities for special needs. For more information contact the publisher.

In Europe, Schiffer books are distributed by
Bushwood Books
6 Marksbury Ave.
Kew Gardens
Surrey TW9 4JF England
Phone: 44 (0) 20 8392 8585; Fax: 44 (0) 20 8392 9876
E-mail: info@bushwoodbooks.co.uk
Website: www.bushwoodbooks.co.uk

Dedication

To all collectors of vintage fabric who share their finds via the Internet.

Acknowledgments

Thank you to: my mother Cynthia, for teaching me to sew, which engendered my love of vintage fabric; my children Sasha and Matthew, for not concluding I was crazy *all* the time while I hunted for fabric; and my husband Paul, for withholding his true feelings as terry cloth overtook our home.

With additional thanks to *Simplicity*, *McCall*, *Vogue*, and *Butterick* for permission to show images of their vintage patterns. Final thanks go to the contributors of images and information to the book.

Supertex advertisement featured in *Australian Home Journal*, November 1960.
Courtesy of Elizabeth, www.vintagefabricaddict.com

Oh, what a merry time is Supertex

TERRY TIME

Make these fresh young fashions in colourful, cool Supertex Terry!

So *naturally* carefree — easy to sew! Such fresh, sunny colours — eye-catching designs! That's Supertex Terry. Wears wonderfully, washes beautifully. Fine towelling texture never shows a hint of a crease — reverse side is smooth for cool-wearing comfort. Pick a pattern — then make it up in cool, colourful Supertex Terry Towelling — it's terrific!

Terry Towelling by **SuperTex**

Contents

foreword

I HAVE loved, collected, and sewn with vintage fabric for more than a decade now. I've noticed over the years that the vintage fabric market cycles through trends, just like different fashion eras from the past inform and inspire today's designers. For a while atomic-era barkcloth is in, then the next year it's all about '30s feedsacks, and the next we're on to '60s European juvenile prints. Terry cloth is soft, cushy, and fun. The heyday of its manufacture also coincided with a particularly stellar era of print design. Whether meant for the kitchen or bathroom, or for a maxi dress or romper, terry cloth was printed with all kinds of vibrant, modern motifs.

Schiffer Publishing's vintage fabric and fashion books are a treasured part of my fabric design library. Whether it's a fabric type, motif type, or era getting the Schiffer treatment, you can trust that it will be comprehensive and inspiring, and that it will be a book you will reference many times over throughout the years. Time and again they have made me look at fabrics from the past in a new way. The same can be said for Monique — I originally met her online and we bonded over our mutual love for vintage fabric. She has an amazing depth and breadth of knowledge regarding textiles of the past, so it's just perfect that she has teamed up with Schiffer for this treatise on vintage terry cloth.

All it takes is one visionary sewist to put a type of fabric in the proper context to start the next vintage fabric trend. Monique was the first, and most fervent, vintage terry cloth champion; and, after spending time with her via these pages, you will be too. It speaks to her enthusiasm and generosity that's she's willing to brave more eBay bidding wars in order to spread her "love of the loop"!

Kim Kight
Author, *A Field Guide to Fabric Design*
Editor, TrueUp.net

New Terry Cloth Robes Get Glamour Treatment in Variety of Silhouettes

1. Exciting new terry cloth peignoir model is made of the different gold imprinted material. 2. One of the most feminine and flattering of the new robes features the cape collar with fringe edge. 3. Extremely wide bath coat is made of the tattersall printed terry cloth. It ties high at the neck. 4. Robe in coat silhouette is cut with raglan sleeves and trimmed with bands of contrasting color. 5. The short coat is designed for beach and play clothes. 6. Decoratively designed loose duster type of coat is trimmed with scalloped edging of gingham, down the front. These sketches from eastern style centers represent fashion trends. The exact models shown may not be available at present, but you will find similar styles now in Spokane stores.

Advertisement in *Spokane Review*, January 1952.

"Terry Cloth"

1925 Favorite for Bathing Robes and Capes

LIKE a rough and ready bath towel this fabric is—but how glorified! The fashionable Miss who wraps herself in its comfort and lightness may well shrug her shoulders at sun and breeze and smart beach gatherings.

Beach Robes

Tailored styles, with long sleeves. Two pockets. Rolled collar. Silk braid binding cord at waist with tassel. Light blue and tan combinations; also mauve and tan. 14.95.

Bathing Capes

Well made and becoming for beach wear. 8.95, 11.95 and 16.95, according to size.

—Second Floor.

Telephone the Shopping Service—Plateau 6261

Beach Capes and Robes in Terry Cloth
Special 8.95

You will be glad of a beach cape in your procession from cottage to bathing beach.

At this special price are beach robes of reversible fancy woven striped terry that will withstand sand and water.

Cowel collar single button neck fastening. Colors— Pink and blue, black and gold, sky and sand, mauve and white. Special 8.95.

Others at 16.95 to 19.95.

—*Second Floor*

Robes
3.95

Terry Cloth

Smarter Than Ever —
Better in Price —

This bath robe special takes the right of way. Absorbent, not too heavy, they have a smartness you don't often find in a terry bath robe, and yet look at the price.

Stripes, self colors and fancy patterns. All have deep pockets and long shawl collars. Green, blue, orange, sand, peach, mauve, wine. Small, medium, large.

Morgan's—Second Floor.

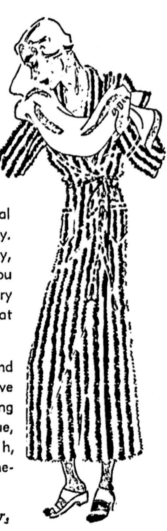

Advertisement for Eaton's, June 1932.

Advertisement for Eaton's, June 1934.

EATON'S

Offers You Tomorrow's Fashions TODAY

TERRY CLOTH BEACH PYJAMAS

DRY OFF in cool, absorbent terry cloth.

SHOW OFF one of these smart color combinations: white trimmed with blue or brown; also plain shades of blue, green or canary.

12.50

MEN'S FURNISHINGS DEPARTMENT,
"Just Inside the Door"
MAIN FLOOR. ST. CATHERINE ST.

T. EATON C⁰ LIMITED
OF MONTREAL

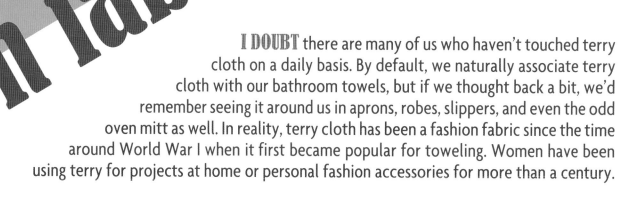

fashion fab(ric)!

I DOUBT there are many of us who haven't touched terry cloth on a daily basis. By default, we naturally associate terry cloth with our bathroom towels, but if we thought back a bit, we'd remember seeing it around us in aprons, robes, slippers, and even the odd oven mitt as well. In reality, terry cloth has been a fashion fabric since the time around World War I when it first became popular for toweling. Women have been using terry for projects at home or personal fashion accessories for more than a century.

Yet terry cloth was still experienced as a relatively plain and functional household fabric until lives and outlooks improved after the hardship of World War II. With pent-up desire for new fashions and decor, soft, comfortable terry cloth became *the* new medium for showcasing beachwear designs. Then came the colorful mod and pop art explosion of the '60s. The bold and vibrant fabric patterns of the period captured the hearts of a whole generation, and encouraged designers to take terry away from the beach and into the streets. Yes, there was a time not so long ago when terry cloth was quite fashionable — even for men! ...Don't believe me? Sean Connery as James Bond wore a blue terry romper in Goldfinger when he was pleasantly surprised by the woman of eventual golden misfortune on the balcony of his hotel room.

With this book, *Terry Cloth*, I will provide a basic history of the origin of the fabric and its manufacture; care hints and sewing techniques; vintage advertisements and sewing patterns; actual attire and decor images; a bounty of resources, including yardage sources; and, most importantly, several hundred glorious fabric photographs...of which, not a single one is a towel!

Incidentally, terry cloth has seen many name variations in usage, including terrycloth, terry fabric, toweling, and terry toweling. For consistency in the book, I will refer to the fabric as terry or terry cloth.

Advertisement for Star & Crescent Mills Co., 1890.

Advertisement for Rubdry Towels, 1911.

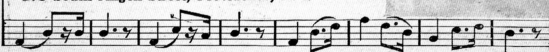

It Promotes Circulation

After exercise, a rubdown with a RUBDRY (dry friction or cold bath) brings a glow of vitality which is restful to nerves and muscles.

THE NEW
RUBDRY
BATH TOWELS
Bath Towel

Guaranteed for 1½ years

RUBDRY Bath Towels are made in 5 sizes (each in an individual box): 39c, 53c, 73c, 85c and $1.25. We recommend the 53c (medium) and 85c (large) sizes as giving best values.

Get a pair (53c or 85c size) of RUBDRY Towels today from your drygoods man, druggist or men's furnisher—or direct from us—and enjoy the real luxury of a rub-down

1 Sample washcloth, 4c to pay postage. Demonstration chart free.

RUBDRY TOWEL CO.
181 So. Angell St., Providence, R.I.

Advertisement for Rubdry Towels, 1911.

Advertisement for décor terry cloth at Gimbel's, August 1925.

GIMBEL BROTHERS

MILWAUKEE   PHILADELPHIA   NEW YORK

A Drapery Sensation!

New Fall Terry Cloth

A Special Purchase! Now
A Sale of 2,000 Yards
Terry Cloth

In Gorgeous and Entirely New Designs

See the Gorgeous Colorings! The Unique Designs! Then Marvel at the Very, Very Low Price

69c Yd.

We've never seen anything like it. And we know you haven't either. Beautiful quality terry cloth—in brand new designs shown for the first time in Milwaukee—at the unbelievably low price of 69c. Terry cloth that you will find suitable—and admired—for almost any room: sun room, living room, dining room or bedroom. Look a few months ahead—and buy now. You'll not regret it.

The dry bit — luckily, we're talking about terry cloth!

In your younger years did you pretend to be a superhero with a towel tied around your neck to form a cape? Or a princess with a towel partially rolled into a doughnut so the tail could hang as a veil down your back? Many a child around the backyard pool has wrapped, dried, and warmed themselves with a curious fabric whose modern identity is closely tied to its fiber — cotton.

No one really knows how long cotton has been used as a textile fiber. Remnants well over 7,000 years old have been found in ancient caves and pyramids. The cotton plant is native to the Americas, but it was generally used less than woolen fibers in Pre-Columbian cultures. Cultivation in the United States mostly grew from influences coming out of the British empire. India had long been the source for the best fibers and fabrics, but the southern American colonies established a new growing region that eventually extended to Texas with the post-independence westward expansion. Native American varieties with longer and stronger fibers gained preference, as did pricing based on the ubiquitous plantation system.

Cotton growing, picking, and processing was labor-intensive well into the 1800s. Although fibers were first spun by machinery in England in 1730, and more quickly processed with the spinning jenny of 1764 and spinning frame of 1769, it was the cotton gin (abbreviated from engine), patented in 1794, that truly introduced cotton to the Industrial Age. As a result, much larger quantities of cotton fiber could be prepared for burgeoning populations that preferred the pricing of cotton over linen and the comfort of cotton over wool.

Today, the world uses more cotton than any other fiber, natural or synthetic. However, during the late 1960s to late '70s, cotton lost its dominance in the textile market for a while as manufacturers lauded the easy-care qualities of the new polymer fibers made from petroleum — the most successful of which was polyester. Popular culture and persuasive advertising assured that modern women needn't worry about shrinkage or ironing ever again. Nevertheless, the one thing most of those synthetics lacked was comfort. They felt coarse and plastic on the skin, didn't breathe well or shed moisture in the summer sun and humidity, and were prone to static discharge in the dry winter months.

One predominantly cotton fabric that maintained its vitality throughout the age of double-knits was terry cloth. The fabric side of the cotton industry definitely benefited from the continued need for toweling — and who could argue with its comfort?

Terry cloth, funnily enough, did not get its name from a guy named Terry ... no matter what you read on the Internet. In the 1906 publication *Textiles and the Origin of Their Names*, a derivation is provided: "Terry Cloth — A pile fabric, with the loops of the pile drawn through a foundation and uncut. From the French term, *tirer*."[1] *Tirer* or *terre* means to draw or pull, as the threads are drawn or pulled to create a loop.

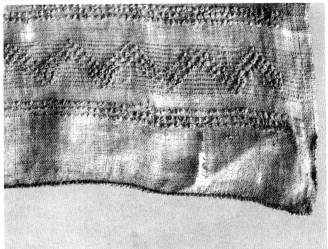

Terry weave cloth believed to have been used by the ancient Egyptians as towels as early as 4000 B.C.
Image from The Buying and Care of Towels and Sheets, Education Department, Cannon Mills, Inc.

Terry Cloth, according to the *Dictionary of Textiles*, ".... is woven with two sets of warp and one filling, one warp forming rows of loops on the face or back or on both sides, which are not cut. It comes bleached, dyed, in colored patterns or printed. The loop piles can cover the entire cloth or form patterns. It can be made from cotton, linen, wool or silk and be used for a great variety of purposes. Main use is for towels and bathrobes, etc."[2]

Throughout much of our history, the world dried off after bathing with a plain-woven, napless piece of cloth, namely huck or huckabuck toweling. Today most of the world uses a variation of Turkish toweling that we now call terry cloth.

In the 1600s, the Ottomans, famed for their carpet-weaving, introduced a new weave to the common towel. Technically, they made a 2/2 twill weave with an extra warp yarn that was looped to form a pile. This meant their towels had a warp and weft (like any cloth), but also a pile of raised yarn loops above the standard flat weave. The loops helped absorb and hold water, which made drying after a bath easier, faster, and more pleasant. An 1872 book on dry goods described it thusly: "Turkish toweling is very coarse and heavy — its principle use is to quicken the circulation of the blood by friction upon the skin. A superior quality of this article is made, having a much larger loop, which is cut at the top, and sheared, thus giving it a soft, downy surface (velour terry cloth). This variety is always bleached, and sold by the yard. It is used principally for ladies' and children's cloaks, gents' summer vests, etc., and is sometimes called 'Terry'."[3]

The first "modern" terry cloth was loomed with silk in France in 1841. In 1845, John Bright, the great statesman of England, began to make worsted terry cloth at his mills in Rochdale near Manchester. The fabric proved to be a great success, and many manufacturers attempted to solve the problem of producing the article in cotton. All failed until Samuel Holt succeeded in making the first cotton terry cloth in 1848. Holt patented his process in England and the United States and, in 1864, Holt left England to found a company and mill in Paterson, New Jersey, to exclusively make terry cloth. Unfortunately, just two years later, the company sold Holt's patents for $250,000. Holt also lost a vast sum of money when he sued the company for breach of contract. An industrial history of Paterson explains the importance of Holt's contribution:

"About thirty years ago, the Sultan of Turkey courteously received an English gentleman and very kindly showed him many hospitable attentions. The gentleman — a member of the firm of Christy & Co., manufacturers of hats — among other things noticed the peculiar round about manner in which the Turkish ladies made the rough kind of towel known to the world as Turkish towels. These towels were highly prized in European countries, and that time commanded a good price. On his return home, the gentleman described to his foreman, Mr Holt, the process practiced in the East of pulling the loops from the cloth by bamboo canes, and hinted to him that the same result obtained by machinery would have many advantages. Mr Holt, after some time, hit upon a plan which, in 1851, was patented in England for fourteen years, and the manufacture of these goods under this patent soon became very remunerative to Christy & Co. They pay an annuity to their old foreman which he still enjoys, and in order to receive further recompense for his own ingenuity, Mr Holt, seven years ago, started the manufacture of "terry" goods, as they are sometimes called, in Patterson, New Jersey. The advantages of this mode of manufacturing are very decided. The loops on each side of the cloth are produced by a peculiar reed motion in the weaving, and as may be supposed, are uniform in length, and the pile of cloth consequently of the same thickness throughout. This style of weaving is applicable to either woolen, cotton or linen fabrics, and is becoming quite popular in towels, tidies, mats, children's dresses, ladies' sacques, upholstery goods, etc. As there is no end to the variety of patterns which can be made, and as many different materials can be used, a manufacturer has at this command a great field for his exertions, and the business has become a staple. Importation in this line has ceased almost altogether since the commencement of the home factories."[4]

SANITARY
Silk Bath Towels.

Made of Pure Uncombed Silk. Producing perfect circulation and invigorating the whole system. One of the greatest reliefs for RHEUMATISM and NEURALGIA. Can be used on the most tender skin, generating a gentle electrical feeling without the least irritation.
WEARING QUALITIES GUARANTEED.
Sent by mail on receipt of price (P. O. order).
$1.00 each; $9.00 per doz.
F. C. SAVAGE & CO.
164 TREMONT STREET,
BOSTON, MASS.,
U. S. A.

Left: An 1891 silk towel advertisement.

Right: A 1911 Martex Turkish towel advertisement.

Samuel Holt was not deterred, as he went on to found S. Holt & Sons in 1872 at Franklin Mill, Pennsylvania, so he could again manufacture Turkish towels. He remained at the mill for one year while employing twelve workers and running six looms. Holt then moved his company to another location after his sons were admitted to the company. At this location, he employed thirty workers, ran fourteen looms with the latest available machinery for the time (most of it imported), and produced between fifty and sixty dozen towels per week.

Turkish toweling slowly caught on, but prior to World War I people weren't willing to part with what they'd always known and used. Huck toweling was readily available from general and dry goods stores in manufactured lengths of a yard. Terry towels did not begin to win overall acceptance until housewives started purchasing them as a substitute for huck towels when the U.S. government commissioned mills to solely make huck towels for servicemen overseas. At the same time, the government issued a 40% duty on any imported terry cloth so locally made cloth was encouraged as the sensible alternative. By the end of the war, huck towels had lost their favor. Thereafter, they were mostly used in kitchens, although terry towels made inroads there as well. From that time on, terry cloth became the predominant personal care fabric, with qualities that increasingly piqued the interest of the fashion world.

To understand how terry cloth is woven, first picture a typical plain-weave fabric of two yarns — one warp lengthwise and one fill (or weft) crosswise. On a loom, the fill yarns are passed over and under the warp yarns and offset by one warp yarn with each pass.

The difference between a plain weave and a terry weave is that the latter, in its simplest form, has three yarns. It still has the plain-weave foundation, but an extra adjacent warp yarn is added, which is loosened and pulled repeatedly to form the loops on one side of the fabric. The density and height of the loops, of course, form the pile.

Most terry cloth is woven on a specialized dobby loom that provides greater control of the tension on yarns in the manufacturing process. A jacquard loom is used to create patterns with multicolored yarns instead of printing dyes and inks.

Depending on the width of the yarns and depth of the pile used throughout the weave, terry cloth is classified as lightweight, medium weight, or heavyweight. Lightweight terry is used for clothing, kitchen tea towels, and poorer quality bath towels. Medium weight terry is used for slippers, bath mats, robes, and standard towels. Heavyweight terry is used for luxurious robes and towels.

Incidentally, terry cloth is still made on hand-looms in Turkey. Hand-woven Turkish towels fetch a princely sum because the weaver can only complete three to four towels every few days.

Enlarged view showing how the loops in terry are formed by the loosening of pile (lengthwise) threads.

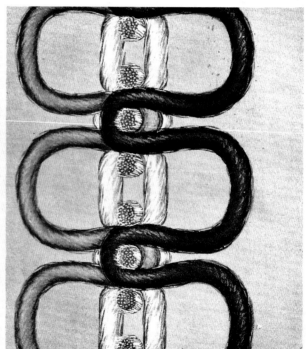

Cross section showing how terry loops are formed on both sides at the same time.

Image from The Buying and Care of Towels and Sheets, Education Department, Cannon Mills, Inc.

Standard cotton terry cloth is woven with loops on one or both sides. It is used for towels or apparel in various weights and qualities. It does not stretch.

French terry is usually constructed of a jersey knit with loops pulled to one side only. It can be made of cotton, bamboo, linen, silk, or rayon, and is usually blended with spandex or polyester to allow stretching. Although technically different, French terry and knit terry are often used interchangeably because they superficially look the same and tend to have varying degrees of stretch.

Knit terry cloth has a plated knit (think double knit) of two interlocked yarn layers that form the front and back of the fabric. One yarn will show on the looped side and the other will show on the smooth or ground side. Typically made of cotton, knit terry can also be made from bamboo, linen, or rayon with added spandex.

Standard cotton velour terry is essentially the same as standard terry cloth except that the loops on one side are sheered to form a flat pile of fur-like yarns. Both sides are not cut to prevent the loop yarns from falling out and maintain the better absorbency of the remaining looped side. **Knit velour** is made the same way as knit terry cloth.

Micro terry is made from polyester micro fiber with very fine, tightly woven loops on one or both sides. It can be found with small to large loops for anything from absorbent cloths to apparel. It can also be found in velour or fleece versions.

Note: For purposes of apparel other than robes, lightweight terry cloth is preferred over heavyweight, but the more important factors in terms of comfort and quality are a higher number of yarns per inch and a higher density of loops. These attributes should be sought in towels as well. Rough terry cloth is the result of poor quality cotton, harsh processing, and low yarn/ loop density.

Typical unwashed standard cotton terry fabric showing loops on both sides. The grain is visible on the unprinted back side.

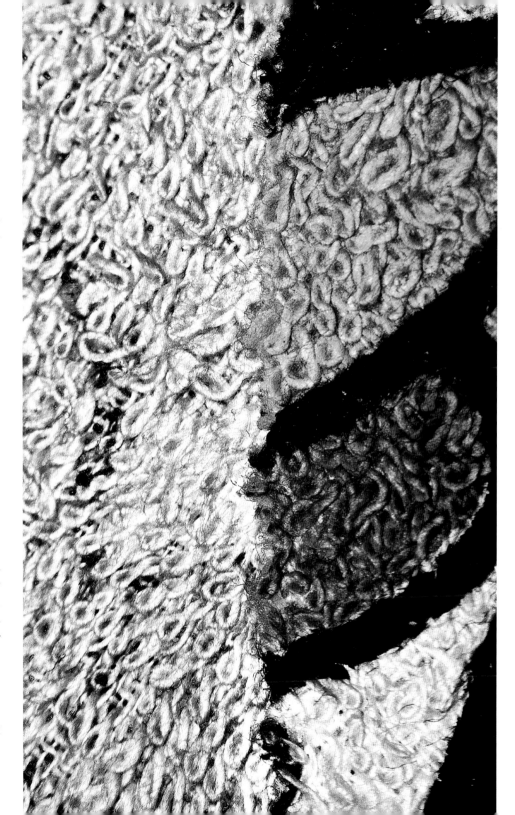

Prior to using and/or wearing terry cloth, it should be washed. Since it will most likely be made of cotton, shrinkage will be a factor to some degree, especially with raw fabric intended for use with a pattern. Washing will remove any sizing on the fabric or any manufacturing residue. It will also strengthen the fibers, tighten the weave, fluff out the pile, and allow the pile to absorb more moisture.

Terry cloth apparel can be washed with towels as long as chlorine bleach and fabric softener are minimized. Super-sterilized and slightly faded bathroom towels are fine, but you wouldn't wish that on your clothes. Hot to cold water can be used, but bear in mind that heat will also take its toll on color and fibers over time. Keep fabric softener to a minimum as it will coat the fibers to soften them, yet make them less absorbent. Hard water, naturally, will add stiffness to the fibers, so softening water is a trade-off. Thorough rinsing is important as always.

After washing, items can be hung outside to dry or placed in a dryer. (Who doesn't love the 'snap' when folding a line-dried towel!) High heat will provide the expected quick-drying cycle, but again moderate heat will prolong the life of the fabric. Also, remember that dryer sheets will add silicone to the fibers, which will actually tend to make them less soft and absorbent.

If you snag a loop or two, don't panic. Just carefully trim the pulled loop back to the outer level of the normal loops. The loose end will be invisible in the dense pile anyway. By not cutting down to the level of the base weave, you'll prevent the yarn from loosening and eventually unraveling.

Velour towels are typically less absorbent than looped terry towels because the water-retaining loop end has been removed. To improve absorbency, soak your towels in hot water with one to two cups of Epsom salt for half a day and then give them a normal wash.

Shake terry towels vigorously when taking from line.

Image from The Buying and Care of Towels and Sheets, Education Department, Cannon Mills, Inc.

Dan River terry cloth advertisement from *Sears Catalog*, 1966.

Anyone who has sewn with terry cloth has probably found it to be a bit of a challenge, especially the first time, but a few basic rules can help.

First, a lesson from Cotton Sewing 101. Wash your 100% cotton fabric. This removes any sizing and sets the length of the cotton fibers for accurate pattern cutting. Chances are the fibers will shrink with washing, so it is best to do it before an item is made that has to fit properly.

However, before you wash terry cloth, it is wise to serge, zigzag stitch, or at least pink any cut edges. You'll thank me later, as edges will unravel and fray rather easily if you don't. This is sensible if not washing, as well.

Terry cloth loops have a nap like velvet, which means they tend to lay in one direction. Before cutting your fabric, make sure all of the nap is laying in the same direction. You can easily find the nap by running your hand up and down the fabric until the surface starts to smooth out where the direction is correct. Inversely, going against the nap will tend to darken the fabric and give a rougher appearance. Cutting your pattern pieces so the nap is aligned will ensure that you don't have areas of light/smooth and dark/rough competing with each other at the project's end. I have completed more than one item to discover that a single piece had an upward nap while the rest was down.

Terry may be a bit tricky to cut depending on the thickness and fullness of the pile and its presence on one or both sides. If working with a pattern, it is easier to lay the pattern piece on the terry cloth as usual, but liberally use weights or long quilting pins to hold it in place rather than standard pins. Doubling up your fabric, no matter how careful you are, can result in movement and jagged edges — especially when using scissors. Scissor-cutting can also cause joint stress in the fingers. Trust me, I know! This is a case where a good rotary tool technique can be a blessing.

A sharp universal 90/14 needle will provide the best results with cotton terry cloth. A ball-point 75/11-90/14 knit needle will work well for knit terry cloth.

Set your machine for 8 to 10 stitches per inch and top-thread tension appropriate to the thickness. Use all-purpose or poly-cotton thread for both the top thread and bobbin.

Standard or zigzag feet can lead to snagged loops, particularly with deeper piles — so be careful. A Teflon® foot is a better choice because it allows the fabric to slide easily without catching. However, standard and zigzag feet are fine for low-pile, French, knit, and micro terry cloths. Foot pressure should be high enough to prevent layer slippage while allowing a smooth flow underneath. A little practice with fabric scraps will help with feel and technique.

If using terry cloth as an appliqué, it helps to sew around the inside edge of your piece with a long and moderately wide zigzag stitch before it is cut from the original fabric. This will reduce the amount of fraying. When your piece is removed, you can trim any stray yarns before applying it with a machine satin stitch wide enough to cover your earlier zigzag stitch.

Have you ever tried to unpick terry cloth? It's seemingly like picking up a grain of sand with chopsticks, right? Yet, it's still doable. Concentration, patience, and perseverance are key to preserving your fabric. Unfortunately, if you pull out a loop of the terry cloth rather than your seam thread, you might create a noticeable run in your fabric. More than once I've had to start again with new fabric.

Schenectady Gazette advertisement, May 1951.

After looking at the fabric images in this book, you might think that terry cloth exploded onto the fashion scene during the 1950s and '60s. However, terry has actually been used as a fashion fabric since its inception. Terry towels have always been transformed by enterprising housewives into decor, apparel, and accessory items like slippers, baby bibs, and diapers, or pretty table runners with added embroidery. It certainly hasn't been a material constrained by its default function.

A *New York Times* article that ran in December 1911 reveals that a woman from New York was visiting Paquin's fashion house in France, where she was informed that a blouse she favored commanded a high price because the newly discovered "cloth" was very difficult to obtain. Undeterred, the customer advised the saleswoman that her towels at home would fashion just as lovely a blouse and at less than a quarter of the cost.[5]

Even though early terry towels were rather drab by modern standards, with minimal coloring and no patterning, the late 1800s brought better technology and greater expectations for more vibrant fashion and decor. Color options in white, blue, green, and brown became available — or, if you were very lucky, black. Terry with stripes could also be purchased if one was willing to pay a little more. As written in a cotton goods guide of 1884: "This weave is not confined to the making of fabrics with an unbroken pile surface, but is adopted in stripes for bath towels and wraps, in check and even figures for quilts, combined with color in other effects and also woven alternately in some special cloth with entirely different patterns. The headings, also for the towels, are of a firmer weave and afford great scope for ornamentation."[6]

After the transition to terry toweling around the First World War, cotton terry cloth became the darling of women who wanted an easy-care, textural fabric that epitomized comfort. Terry cloth was wearable at the beach or to the supper club, and irresistible while lounging at home — all while looking good, resisting wrinkles, and absorbing perspiration in a time before the use of everyday deodorants. The vogue for colorful design in household accessories merged with fashion around 1928 to increase the popularity of terry cloth.

As servicemen and women returned from Europe after World War II, they brought a new appreciation for enjoying life to their respective countries. In combination with the growing beach culture sweeping many nations, clothing became less restrictive. A 1949 report from a fashion show stated, "Appropriate for American living and in good taste were the summer fashions shown yesterday... terry cloth, one of the most functional fabrics for the beach, has been adopted on a large scale by fashion designers recently. It appeared on the runway in many shapes and colors."[7]

By the following year, terry cloth was proving to be more than a temporary fad. "From a towel into a swimsuit, beach dress or coat is the long stride terry cloth has taken into the fashion scene. Clever designers seeking new ideas, and alert fabric men are responsible for this. Long aware of the fabric's absorbency and other valuable qualities, they now have used it for resort wear that is new as well as practical and attractive."[8]

At the same time, French designers started featuring the fabric in their resort and sportswear collections. Californians, with their sun-drenched lifestyles, heartily embraced the new designs. The mills were newly producing showy prints that opened eyes much like those in barkcloths seen at the time, but these designs were just a hint of the boldness of a decade later.

Improvements in terry cloth manufacture helped with acceptance in fashion circles. The weave had been tightened and refined with less bulk for apparel production. Color palettes were broadened to a full range of hues in prints and stripes. The development of coordinating fashion items coincided with those of home decor. In an article titled "Toweling Turns to Brighter Hues," printed in the *New York Times* in August 1956, the writer stated: "The main reason for the rise in towel sales in recent years is the growing consumer awareness of the fabric as a fashion accessory. This has created a rate of obsolescence governed by style rather than utilitarian factors." He goes on to say that an industry leader "soon discovered the towels were being used for as much as decorative as utilitarian purposes. Towels were being refashioned into table mats, napkins, curtains, aprons, displayed as pictures in frames and even made into blouses."[9]

What had started with solid colors and a smattering of stripes literally blossomed into prints galore! In the '50s, flowers and botanicals ruled the fabric aisles, with a hint of the geometric and atomic influences seen in barkcloth. The presence of bold solids and geometric styles allowed men to join women in readily accepting terry cloth as a fashion fabric. From the bathroom to lounge and beachwear, terry cloth reflected a more casual culture ready for a decade of stylistic fun. Terry apparel was frequently seen in photographs and film; movie actress Marilyn Monroe was notable for modeling terry beachwear in a few popular pinups.

It is a challenge to determine which major designer gave terry cloth the most favor in the 1960s — the fabric's heyday. Pucci, Lilly Pulitzer, Mary Quant, Vera, and Pierre Cardin all designed for body and home. The fabric was no longer just the stuff of towels. Lightweight terry was fashioned for everyday apparel and dressier outfits as well. Many a star was seen in terry cloth ensembles, including Mattel's fashion-conscious Barbie™.

As mod fabrics became the trend for everywhere except the corporate boardroom, manufacturers followed demand with even bolder designs. By 1971, an *Associated Press* writer wrote: "Terry cloth has been taken out of the bathroom and is doubling for at-home outfits in new jumpsuit designs for Formfit Rogers by Emilio Pucci and Bernice Lang … the lingerie company had begun to line the tops of their nightgowns so they could be worn as evening dresses. Many of the gowns had hooded coats to match and others had pants that could make a lounging pajama or a patio outfit."[10]

As manufacturers began to blend polyester and spandex with cotton terry cloth in partnership with the synthetic-fiber industry, mid-1970s designers abandoned the whimsical prints of the '50s and '60s. Solid colors and stripes returned to apparel fashion, although bathroom and kitchen accessories continued to show the colorful pictorials consumers had fallen in love with. Yet, every couple of years, terry cloth was still being reported as a trendy fabric as if everyone was seeing it in items other than toweling for the first time.

With knitted fabrics all the rage, stretchable terry was the new activewear in bold colors for women and men. A 1977 *Sarasota Journal* article reported: "We were investigating terry cloth, which has advanced insidiously, like a creature in a Japanese science fiction movie. First, it was toaster covers, robes, towels, and bath slippers, but that wasn't enough. Terry reached out to the patio, the tennis court, the beach, and now — is there no stopping it? — it's extending its little loops to whatever-wear: skirts, tops, jumpsuits, whatever you're inclined to wear."[11]

In a 1979 article in the *New York Times,* another writer began: "Terry cloth is out of the bathroom and stepping into the office, the boardroom, and the dinner party. This spring, terry cloth is turning up in dresses, men's and women's blazers, and fashionable tops, and these looks are being worn as both everyday and dressy attire."[12]

Perhaps surprisingly, the influence of terry cloth in men's fashion of the period can't be emphasized enough. A men's fashion editor for *UPI* wrote a 1979 article under the banner "Color Returns to Male Clothes," where he stated: "After several spring seasons in which men's fashions seemed as muted as a rainy April day, 1979's color lovers can celebrate — bright is back. It is not the psychedelic mishmash effect that so marred the '60s, but rather a fancy-free mixture of classics and a dash of bright color that promises to make this one of the most exciting spring fashion seasons in a decade. The leading pilferer from the rainbow is active sportswear, or, as the lords of the fashion world are calling it this year, action-wear. For example, a wide range of terry cloths will soon be filling up the stores, as designers scramble to become recognized as the all-around action-wear maker. This year's athletic wear will run the gamut from brightly colored, cut-down models featuring panels and trims, to fuller cut terrycloth that comes in colors as spectacular as sunburst orange or as mundane as navy blue or sweat-shirt gray. Indian madras, the perennial favorite, makes a strong showing again this spring as does the terrycloth rage, which is truly sweeping the fashion front page."[13]

In the 1980s, the prevalence of synthetic terry cloth fabric diminished as fashion trended toward the use of cotton again. Even 100% cotton terry fabric had become a rarity except for traditional uses in toweling, robes, and slippers. Activewear, long a mainstay of the industry, transitioned to plain knitwear, especially in cotton with spandex.

Terry fabric production remained fairly dormant until 2009 when it found renewed favor with designers, as solids, stripes, and showy prints were revealed in casual clothing and handbags. Thanks to newer fiber technology, current knit terry felt softer, draped flowingly, and didn't pull as easily as it had in the past. In 2010, terry cloth was once again being offered in fun and cute prints. Sources like Juicy Couture, Pucci, Mini Boden, Baby Gap, and Victoria's Secret showed apparel for all ages.

Terry cloth, like any other fashion fabric, has survived crests and troughs of interest. The creative peak for terry cloth fabric design ran from the late 1950s to the mid-1970s. Although production on that scale ceased some time ago, recent years have seen a resurgence in appreciation for the fabulous prints from that era. Every few years terry is explored anew by an up-and-coming designer or revisited by a veteran looking for an alternative look.

A 2010 search of the United States Patent Office records has shown that new processes for improving terry cloth are submitted for patent every few years. Who knows when the next reincarnation of fashion terry will be trendy, with a luxuriant texture and bounty of dazzling designs.

they're terry...
they're terrific...

K-Mart advertisement, 1979.

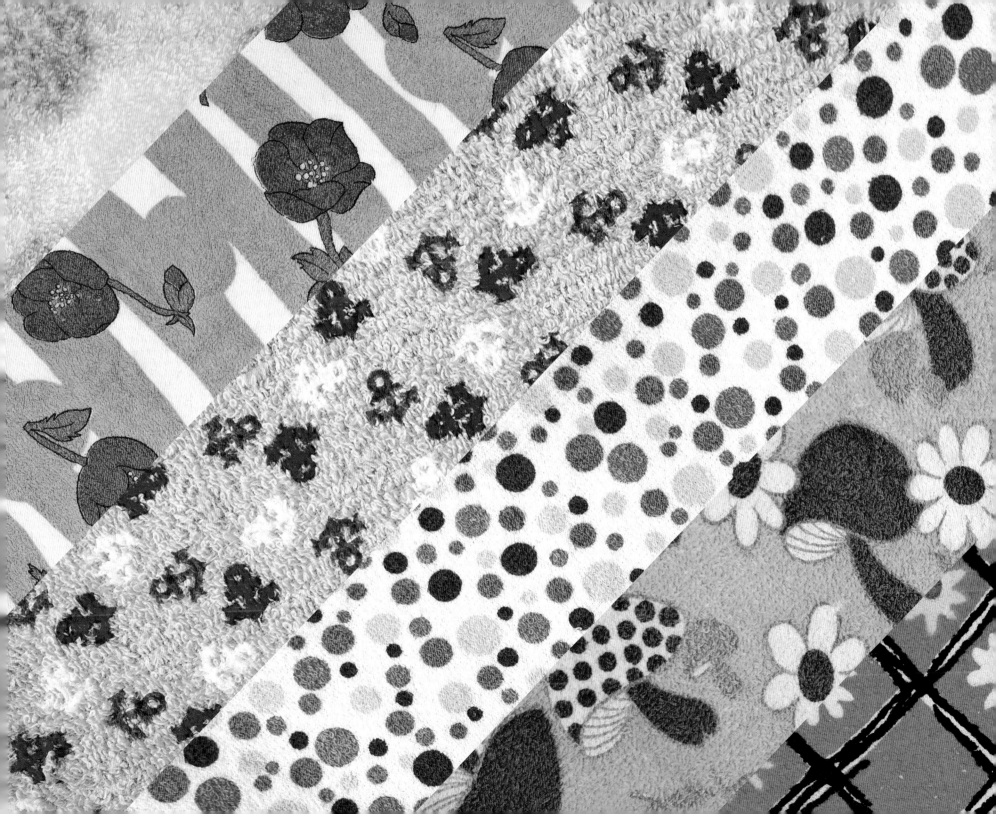

AS WITH every fashion that has trended in the media and stores, terry cloth has been marketed to the home sewer. Please enjoy the following original newspaper, magazine, and catalog ads and then note how the styles have been emulated in sewing patterns and projects devoted specifically to the fabric. The clothing selection shows a mix from fashion shops and home-sewing rooms — and no history would be complete without featuring a "pile" of towels.

Coats & Clark leaflet, circa 1960s.

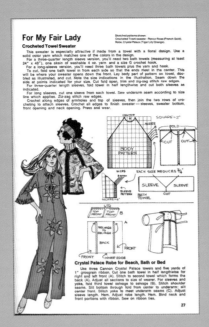

Sweater and robe instruction, 1972.
Image from Love & A Few Stitches, Cannon Mills, Inc.

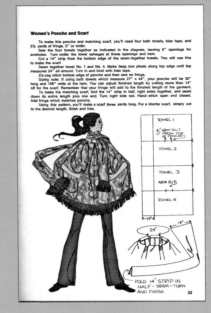

Poncho and scarf instructions, 1972.
Image from Love & A Few Stitches, Cannon Mills, Inc.

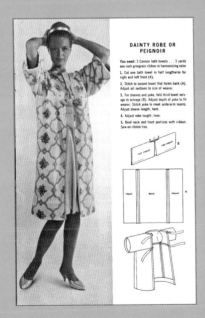

Peignoir instructions, circa 1960s.
*Image from Make it with Towels!
Cannon Homemaking Service,
Cannon Mills, Inc.*

Short and long cover-up instructions, circa 1960s.
*Image from Make it with Towels! Cannon Homemaking Service,
Cannon Mills, Inc.*

Towel skirt instructions, 1972.
*Image from Love & A Few Stitches,
Cannon Mills, Inc.*

A 1972 Cannon Mills, Inc. bedding and bathroom accessories advertisement …

… And the matching outfit! *Image from Love & A Few Stitches, Cannon Mills, Inc.*

Jiffy-Sew!

by Anne Adams

Play-coat or cooler-length wrap-around, with matching shorts beneath! Sew this versatile style in terrycloth for the beach; as a cotton apron, or simply a gay sun and fun outfit! Jiffy-sew (it wraps) opens flat to iron. Make it for summer—right now!

Pattern 4821: Misses' sizes 10, 12, 14, 16, 18. Size 16 wrap 3½ yards 35-inch; shorts 1⅛ yards.

This pattern easy to use, simple to sew, is tested for fit. Has complete illustrated instructions.

Send 35 cents in coins for this pattern—add five cents for each pattern for first-class mailing. Send to Anne Adams. care of The New London Day, 123, Pattern Dept., 243 West 17th St., New York 11, N. Y. Print plainly name, address with zone, size and style number.

4821
SIZES
10—18

Anne Adams mail-order pattern advertised in *The Day*, May 1956.

Create a Terry wardrobe...

If you know how to sew, you can create a wardrobe of carefree fashions from exquisite Cannon Royal Family bath towels. So simple to whip up (see diagram below) and 2 bath towels are all you need.

Choose from the wide assortment of prints, jacquards and solid color fashion towels...in fluffy terry or velvety surfaced terry.

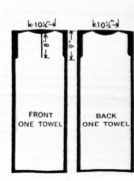

FRONT
ONE TOWEL

BACK
ONE TOWEL

Flower power in Beach Belle terrycloth

2.29 yard

Move swimmingly into summer — with a swim suit and cover-up sun-splashed with flowers. Create them both from all-cotton terrycloth, 45" wide in pool-pretty prints. Or make waves with solid shades in terry velour, **1.89 plain terry, 3.98 velour.**

Other bright prospects: dotted swiss, eyelet, voile, cotton lace, jersey cottons and blends — all specially priced for nary a ripple in your budget.

Simplicity Pattern No. 7645 requires 2¼ yds. for set, ⅝ yds. for suit alone.

FOURTH FLOOR FASHION FABRICS

Fabric advertisement in the *Deseret News* with suggested Simplicity Pattern, June 1969.

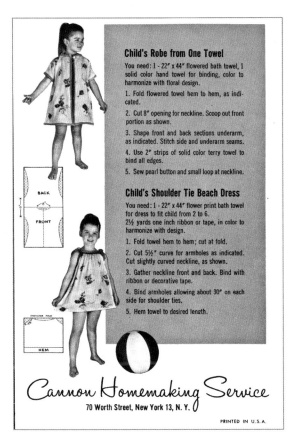

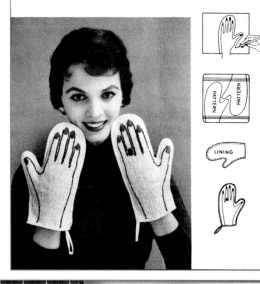

Clockwise from above:
Beachwear leaflet from Cannon Mills, Inc., circa 1960s.

Supertex advertisement featured in the *Australian Home Journal*, November 1960.
Courtesy of Elizbeth, www.vintagefabricaddict.com

Instructions for making oven mitts from washcloths, circa 1960s.
Image from Toys from Towels, Cannon Mills, Inc.

Instructions for making an Afghan from washcloths, 1972.
Image from Love & A Few Stitches, Cannon Mills, Inc.

1960s *McCalls* 7134

1960s *McCalls* 8693

1960s *McCalls* 8738

1960s *McCalls* 9609

1960s *Vogue* 7073

1960s *Vogue* 6751

1965 *McCalls* 8846

1960s *Vogue* 6241   1960s *Simplcity* 8753   1965 *McCalls* 6351

1968 *Simplicity* 7572

1968 *Simplicity* 7648

1969 *McCalls* 9785

1969 *Simplicity* 8141

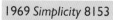

1969 *Simplicity* 8153

1969 *Simplicity* 8244

1969 *Simplicity* 8251

1969 *Simplicity 8551*   1979 *Simplicity 8787*

1970s *Style 2722*

1974 *Simplicity 6431*

2002 Butterick 3474

1960s Butterick 6165

2010 New Look 6882

1950 McCalls 1749

1964 Simplicity 5767

1973 Simplicity 5662

TERRY MAKES MERRY for bath or beach. Bold flowers flourish on thirsty 9-ounce cotton terry. Pink or blue. Sizes 4-6x, $5; 8-14, $6. Kerchief, $1; beachbag, $2. At Neiman-Marcus, Dallas, Houston and Forth Worth; and other fine stores.

Her Majesty®

Neiman-Marcus advertisement in *The New Yorker* showing the original kerchief superimposed, March 1968.

Terry cloth outfits from *National Bella Hess Catalog, 1934. Courtesy of Lauren, www.wearinghistory.etsy.com*

French Finish COTTON LINENE $1.00

TERRY CLOTH $2.39

Florida went wild over this sport pajama. One-piece with bright contrasting cross-strap back, sash and buttons. White with Apple Green; White with Orange or Nile Green with Orange. Women's and Misses' Sizes: 28 to 38 bust. *Not Prepaid.*
7M1254—Terry Cloth. Shpg. wt., 1 lb. 10 oz. $1.98
7M1255—French-finish cotton Linene. Shpg. wt., 1 lb. 2 oz.......... $1.00

COTTON LINENE $1.00

TERRY CLOTH $1.98

Slacks and a swanky jacket—a grand beach costume. Sizes: 28 to 38 bust.
7M1252—French-finish Cotton Linene. Navy, Green or Red double-breasted jacket with White pants. Shpg. wt., 1 lb. 2 oz....Not Prepaid. $1.00
7M1253—Terry Cloth. Navy jacket with White pants; Green with White pants; Orange with Blue pants. Shpg. wt., 2 lbs....Not Prepaid. $2.39

Combination separates of French middy top and snug shorts are styled for play. **Glove-snug terry cloth dry-offs provide fashionable change from bathing suits.**

St. Petersburg Times advertisement, June 1953.

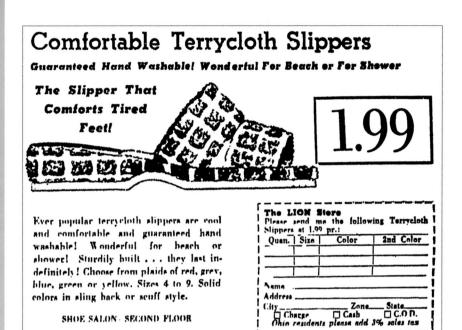

Slipper advertisement in *Toledo Blade*, July 1954.

Ripon magazine advertisement in *The New Yorker*, June 1960.

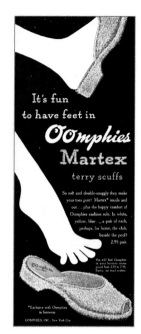

Martex slipper magazine advertisement, circa 1960s.

Slippers and lounge chair covers advertisement in the *Deseret News*, June 1966.

The Pittsburgh Press newspaper advertisement, January 1979.

A 1970s Eaton's catalog depicting swimwear and activewear.

A 1970s Eaton's catalog depicting loungewear and activewear.

A 1970s Eaton's catalog depicting activewear.

A 1970s Eaton's catalog depicting loungewear and activewear.

A 1970s Eaton's catalog depicting menswear.

A 1970s magazine advertisement.

Homemade wrap dress from *Simplicity* 7572.

A 1960s shift dress with applique terry cloth flowers. Stems and grass are printed on fabric. Label unreadable.

Homemade shift dress with back zip closure.

Front snap closure robe with chenille fringe trim.

Homemade tabard with velvet closures on sides

Butterfly jacket.
*Courtesy of Lisa Gerun,
www.vintageflirtygirl.etsy.com*

Front button closure shirt.
*Courtesy of Jacqui Kelly,
www.kittyvonpurr.etsy.com.*

Two-piece lounge suit.
Courtesy of Pat Myers,
www.affairedamourvintage.com.

Pucci. Courtesy of Cynthia Hess.

Maxi dress with terry trim.
Courtesy of Meghan Hayes,
www.eluctantdamsel.etsy.com.

Homemade poncho with
pom pom trim.

Beach jacket.
Courtesy of Dawn Steckmesser,
www.slapsymaxi.etsy.com

Printed romper.
Courtesy of Seasons Clayton,
www.niftygypsyvintage.etsy.com

Courtesy of Deb, www.mrspsbrain.etsy.com.

Printed beach cover-up.
Courtesy of Lisa Gerun,
www.vintageflirtygirl.etsy.com

Front button closure robe.
Courtesy of Meghan Hayes,
www.reluctantdamsel.etsy.com

Homemade front zip closure and
chenille fringe trim.
Courtesy of Dawn Steckmesser,
www.slapsymaxi.etsy.com

Bikini.
Courtesy of Suzie Vazquez,
www.pinupdresses.com

Short mini dress.
Courtesy of Darleen Gillyard,
www.dvgvintage.etsy.com

Bedroom and bathroom coordinates, *Woman's Day* advertisement for St. Marys, October 1970.

Kitchen coordinates, *Good Housekeeping* advertisement for Morgan-Jones, June 1965

A 1975 kitchen coordinates magazine advertisement for Morgan-Jones.

A 1976 kitchen coordinates magazine advertisement for Morgan-Jones.

A 1969 *Pucci* magazine advertisement with modeled harem suit …

… and a 1969 *Pucci* bedroom and bathroom co-ordinates magazine advertisement.

A 1950s bathroom towel set with printed His and Hers design.

A 1960s bathroom towel set with printed gingham floral design.

A 1970s bathroom towel set with printed butterfly design.

A 1970s beach towel.

A 1960s bathroom towel set with printed Poodle design.

A 1960s bathroom towel set with printed His and Hers design.

A 1970s bathroom towel set with embroidered Love design. *Courtesy of Sandra Sharp, www.vintagedame.etsy.com.*

A 1970s kitchen towel.

A 1970s kitchen towel set.

Printed pillows, circa 1970s.

JOIN ME in savoring these diverse and fabulous 1950s to late 1970s fabrics — all but a few from my collection. I hope the designs will surprise, delight, and inspire you as they have me these many years. You will even find a number of fabrics with more than one colorway. From the delicate florals to pop geometrics, they will show a fabric type consistently overlooked in design histories. There really is a lot more to terry than towels ... but please don't feel too envious that I get to cuddle them every day!

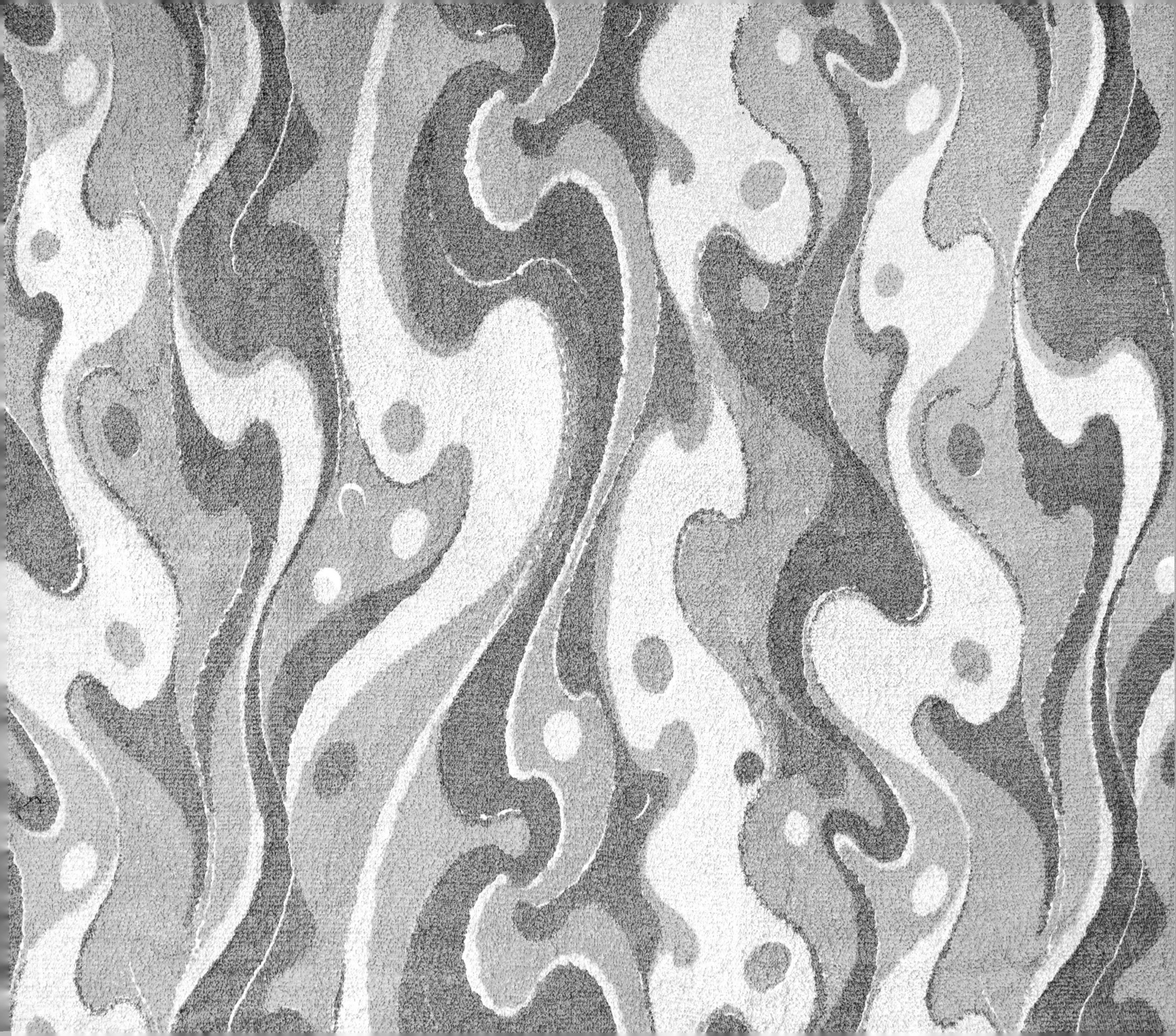

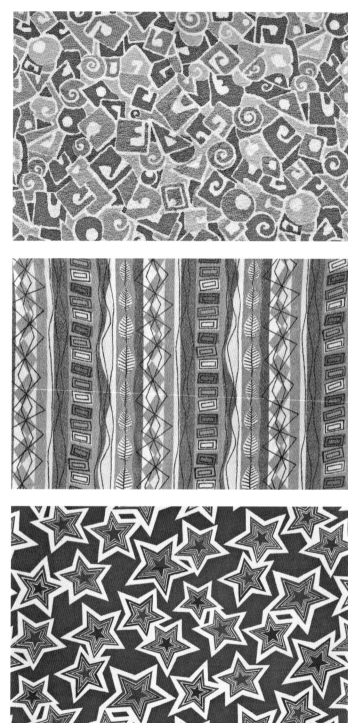

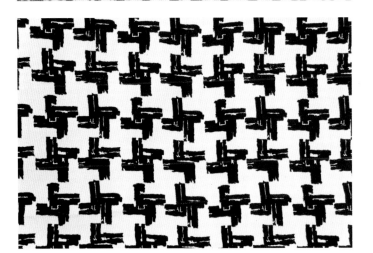

Abstracts & Geometrics

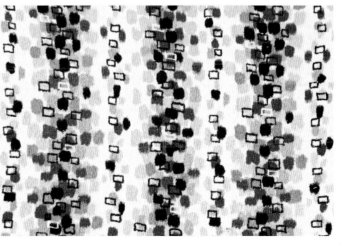

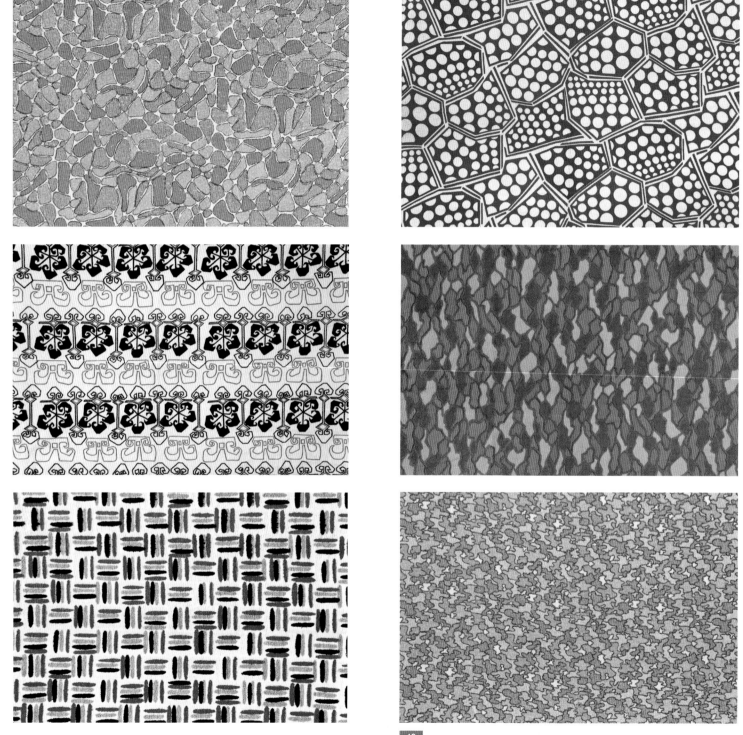

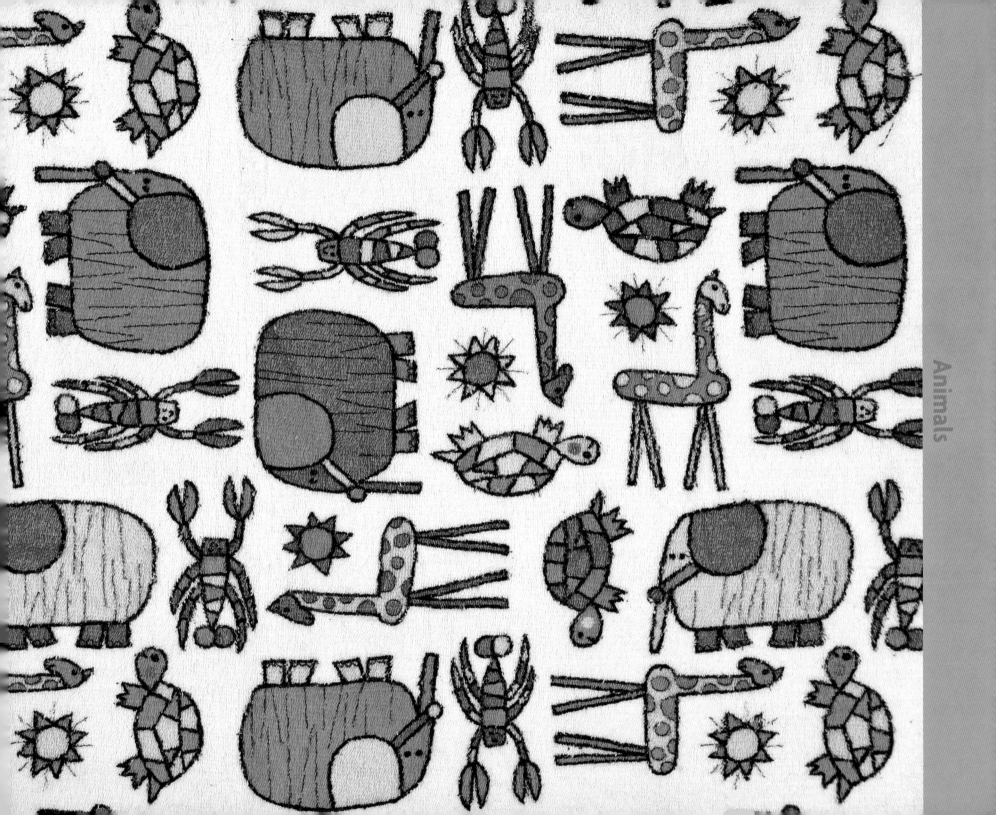

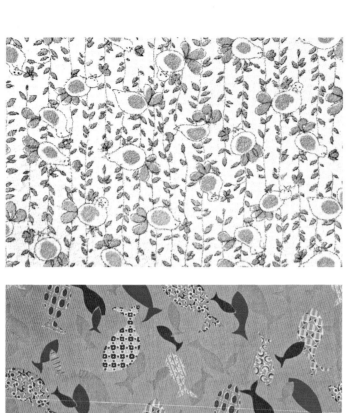
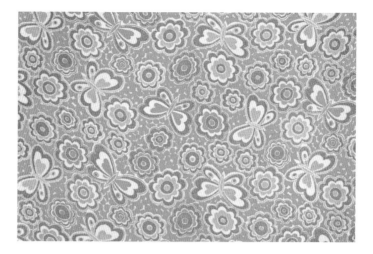

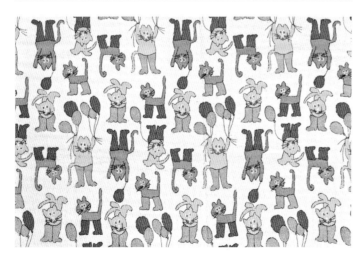

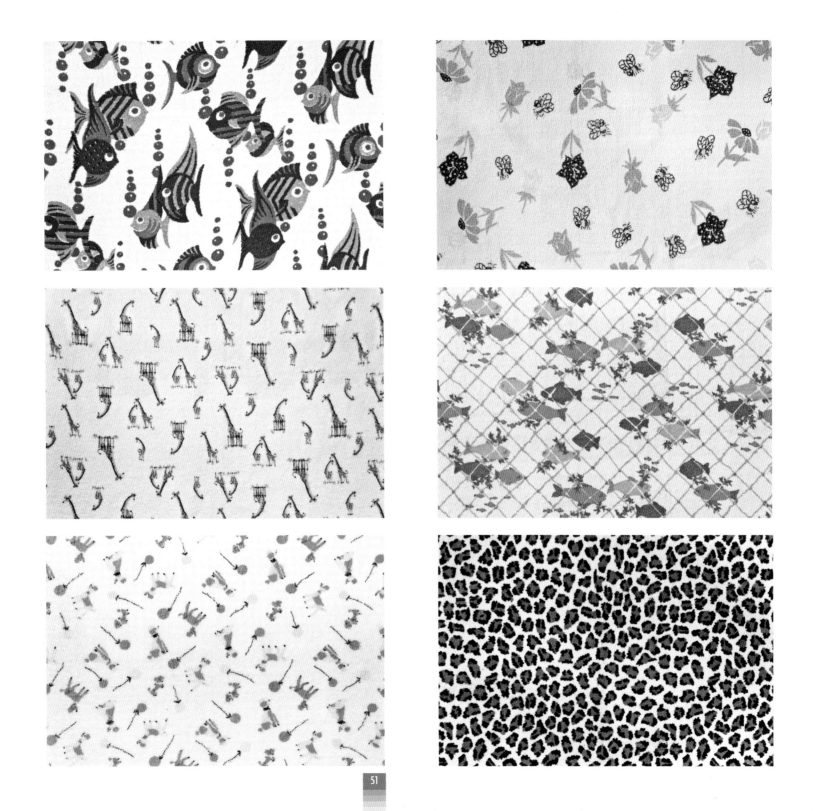

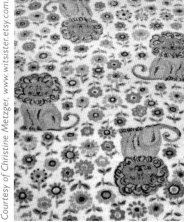

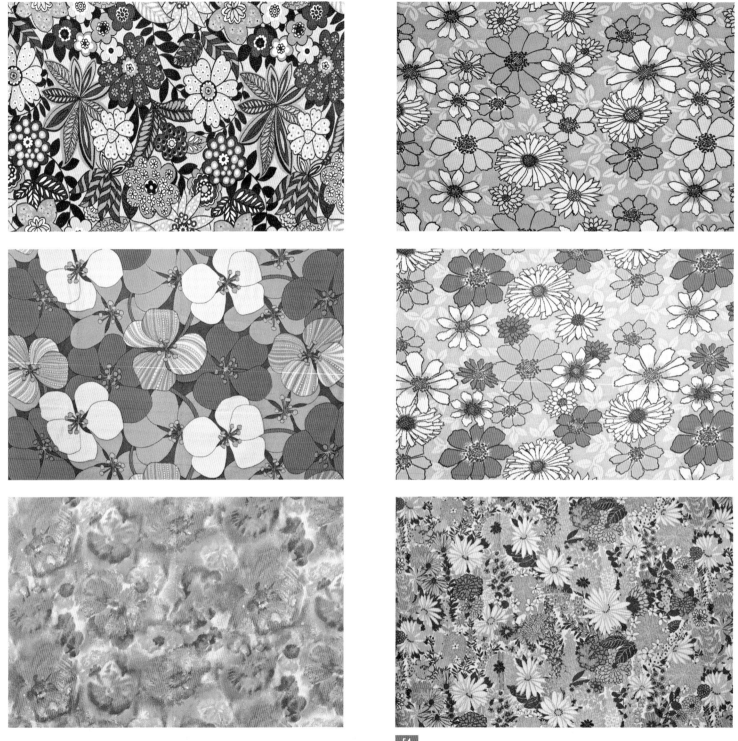

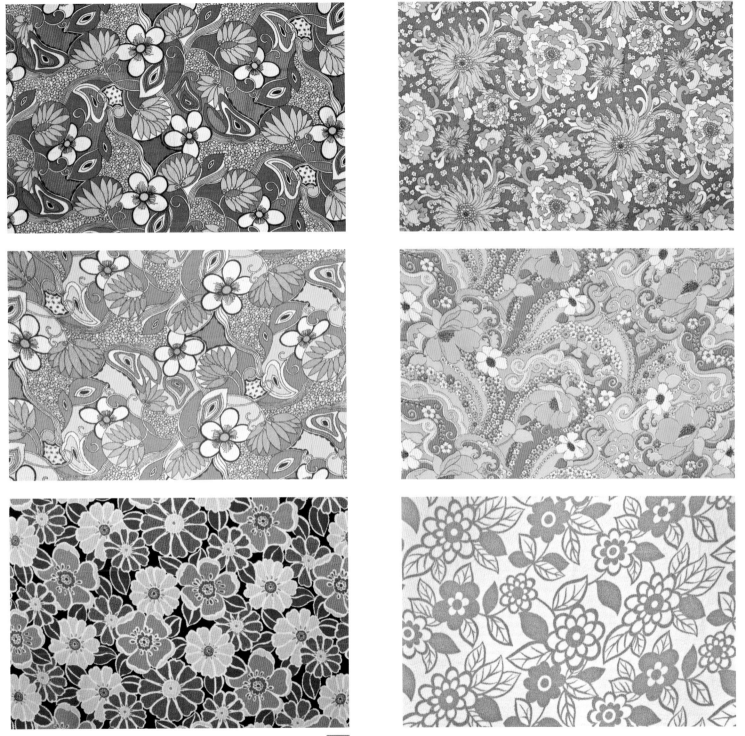

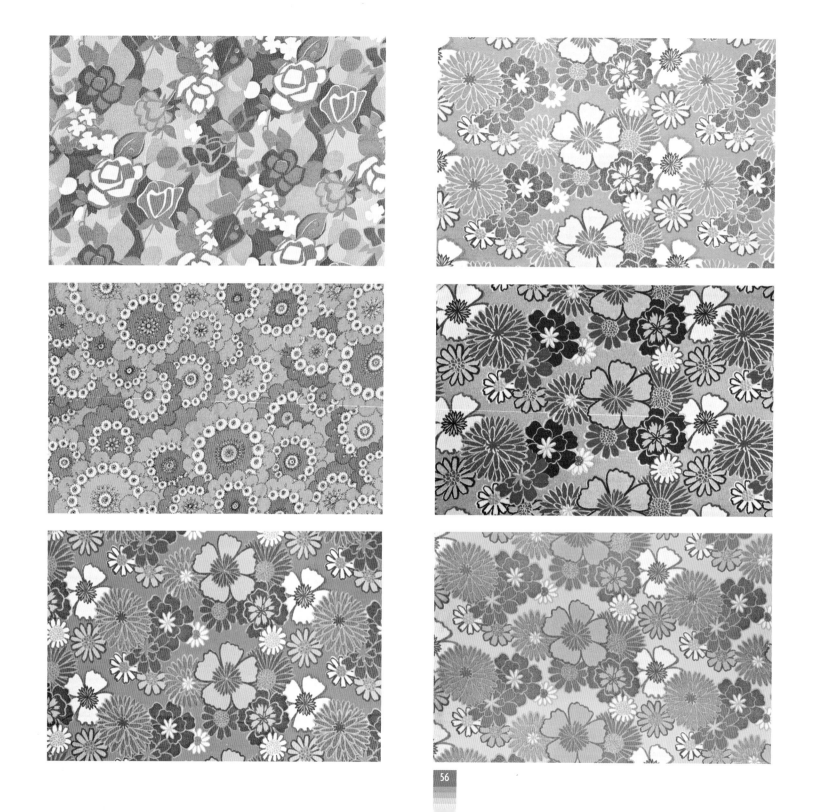

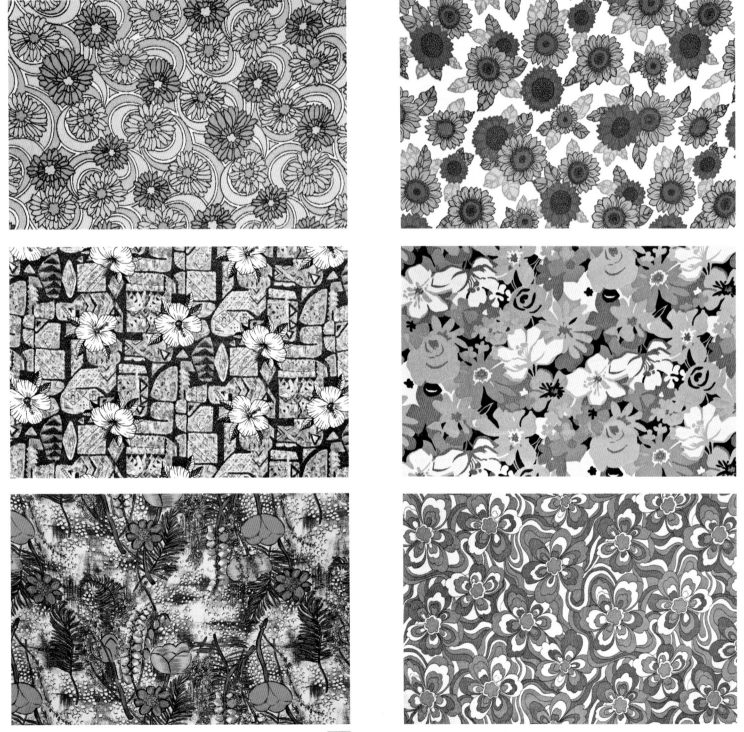

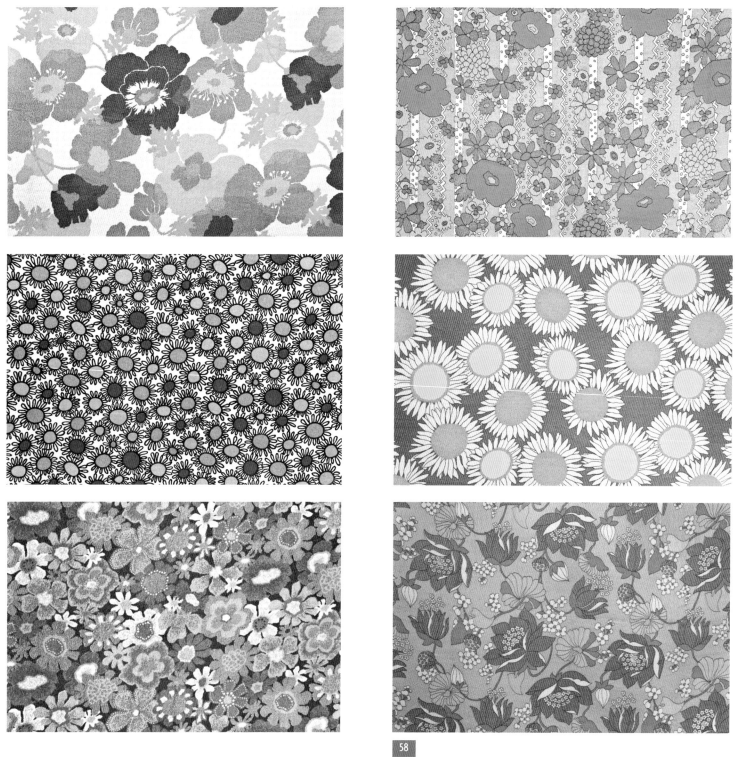

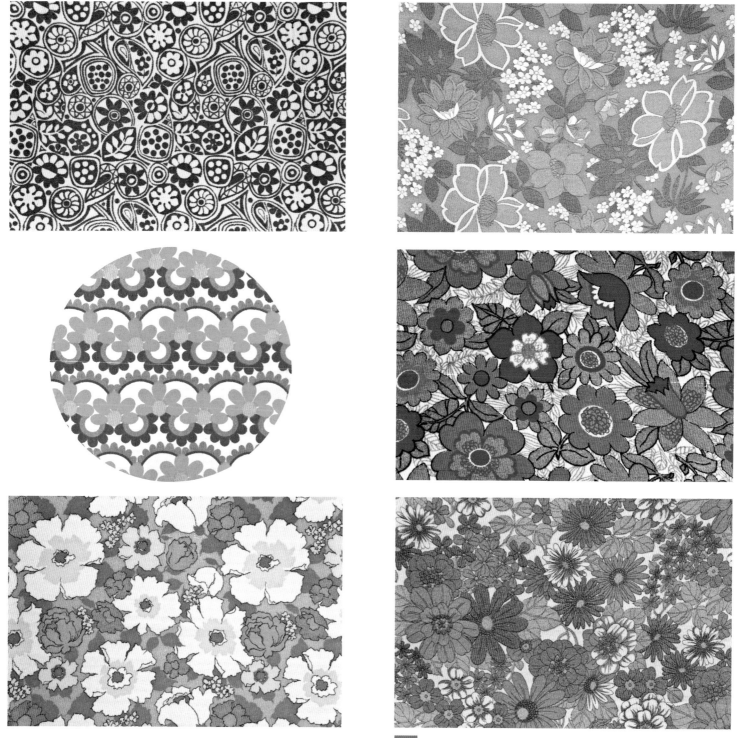

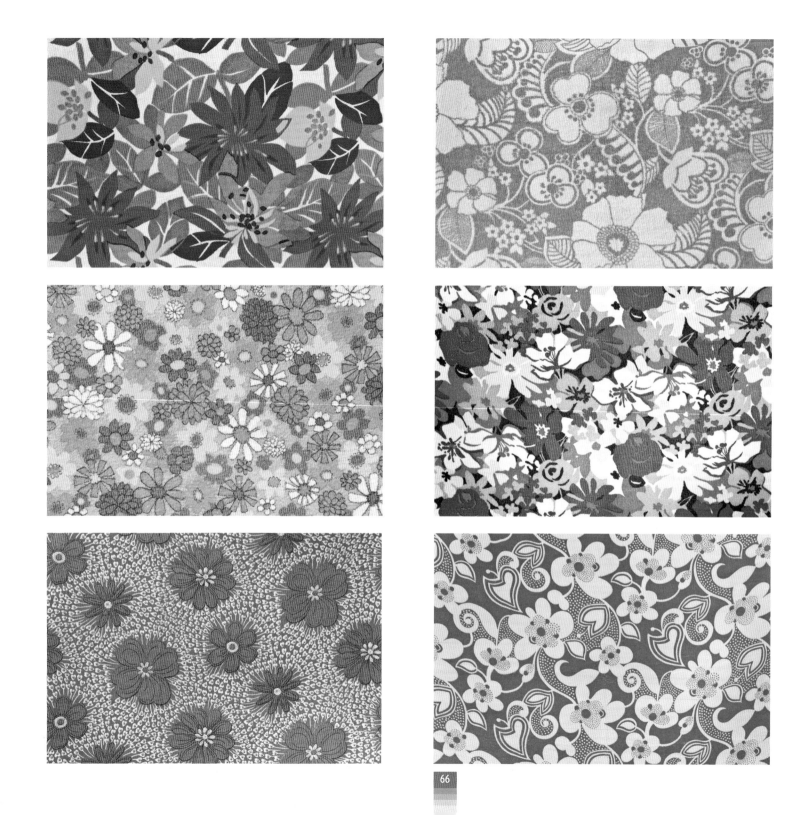

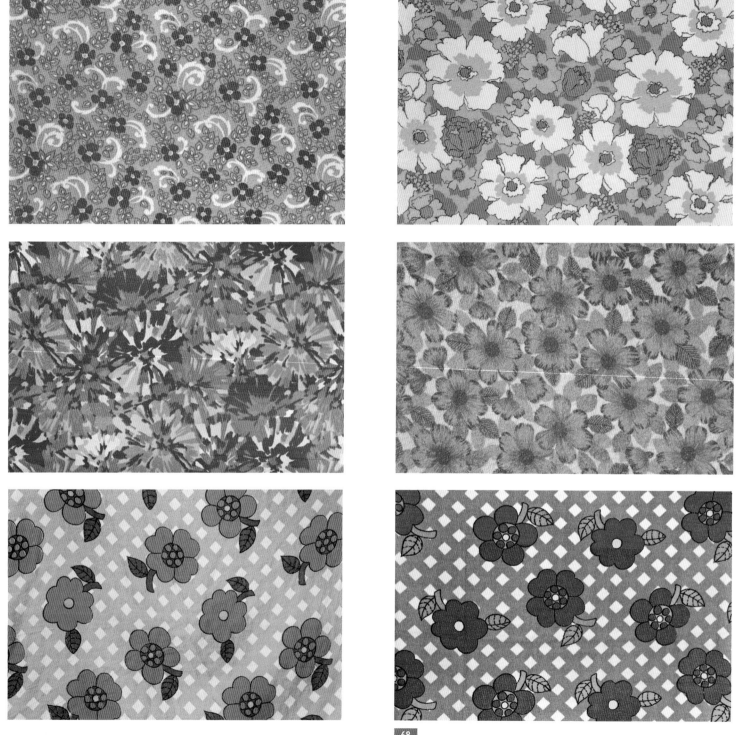

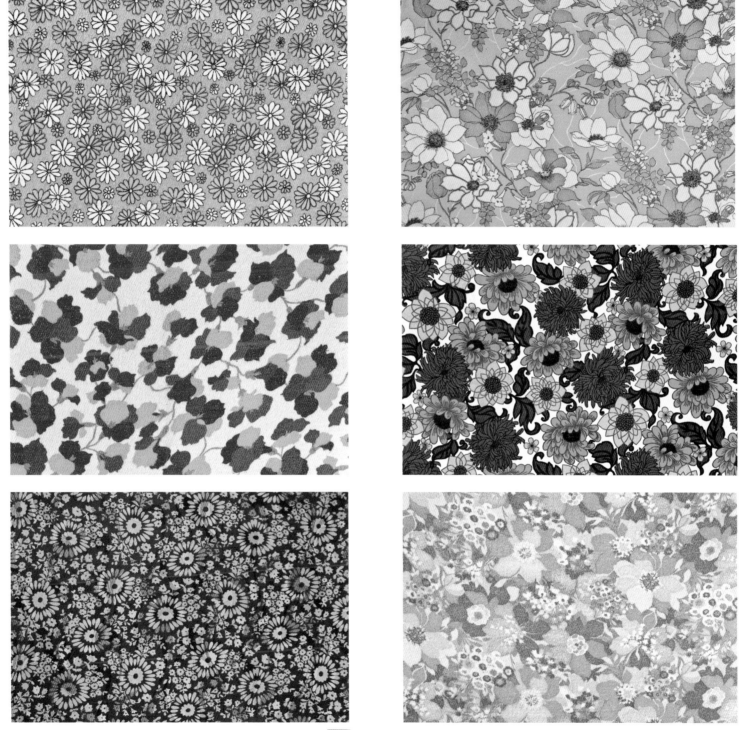

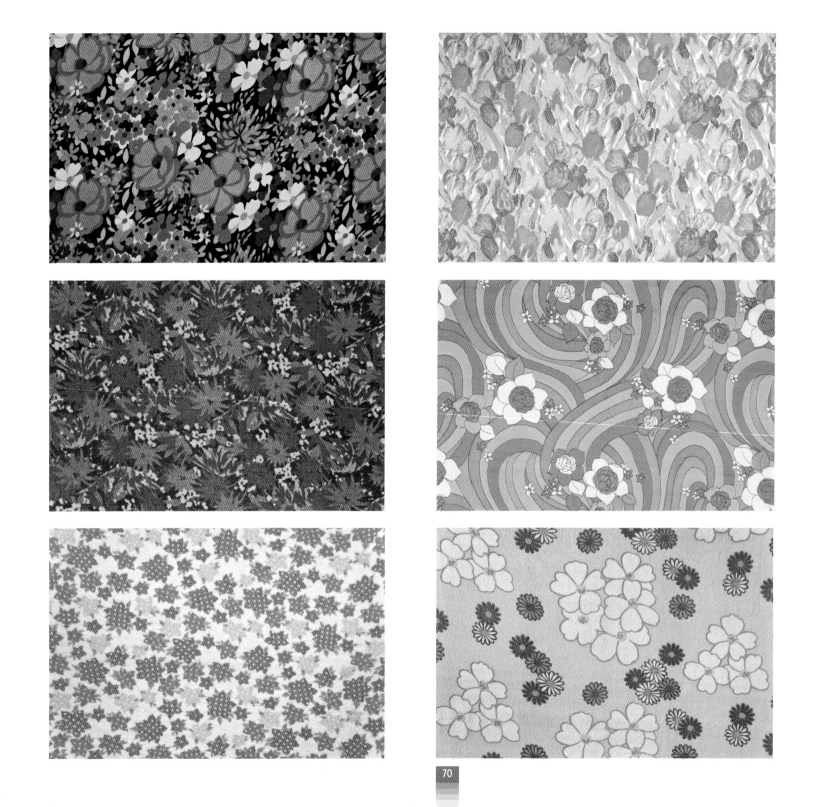

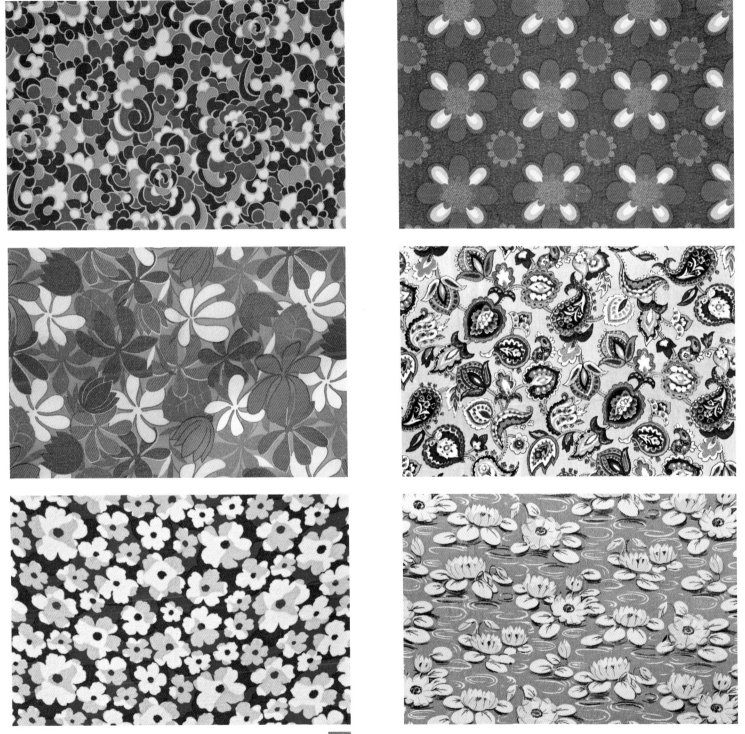

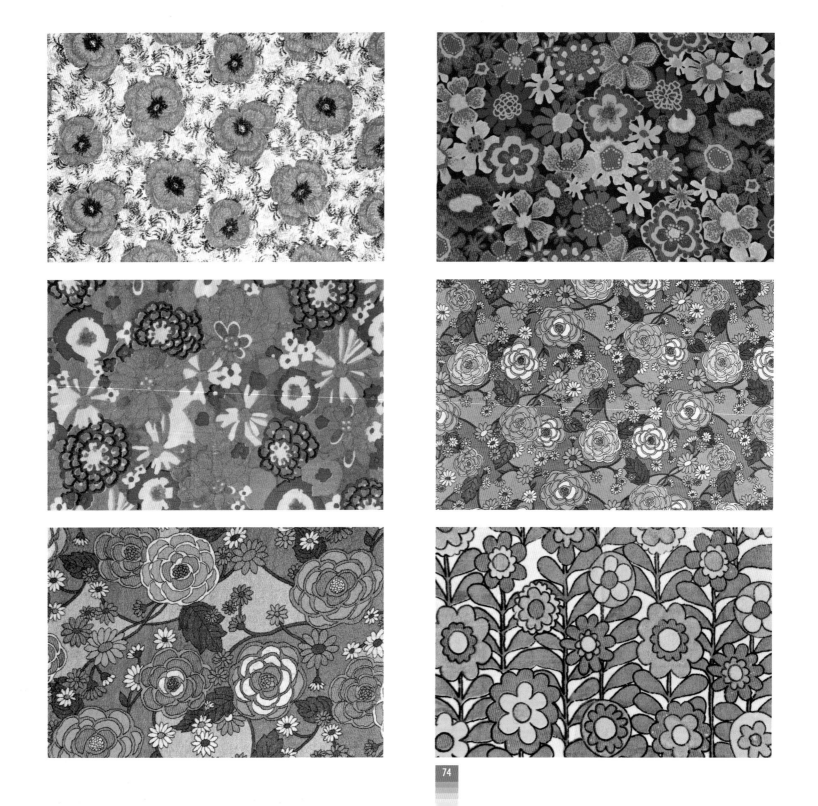

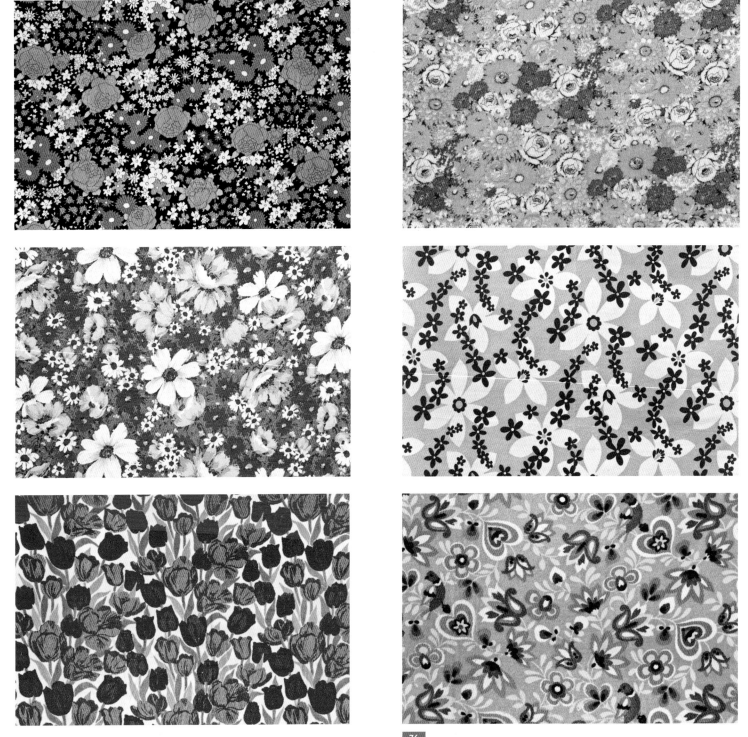

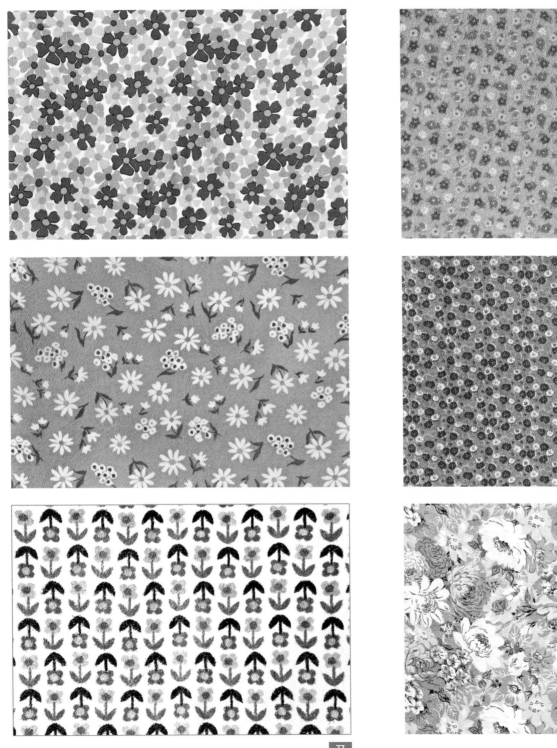
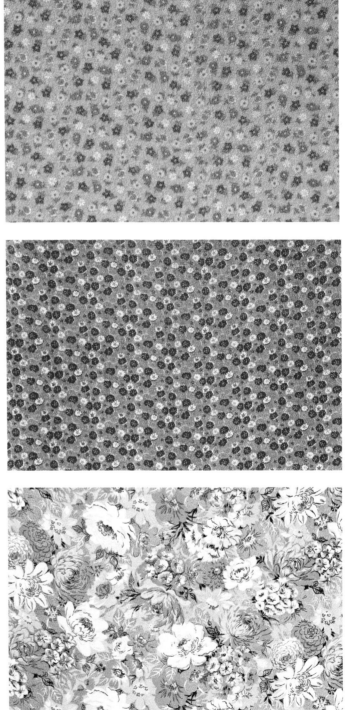

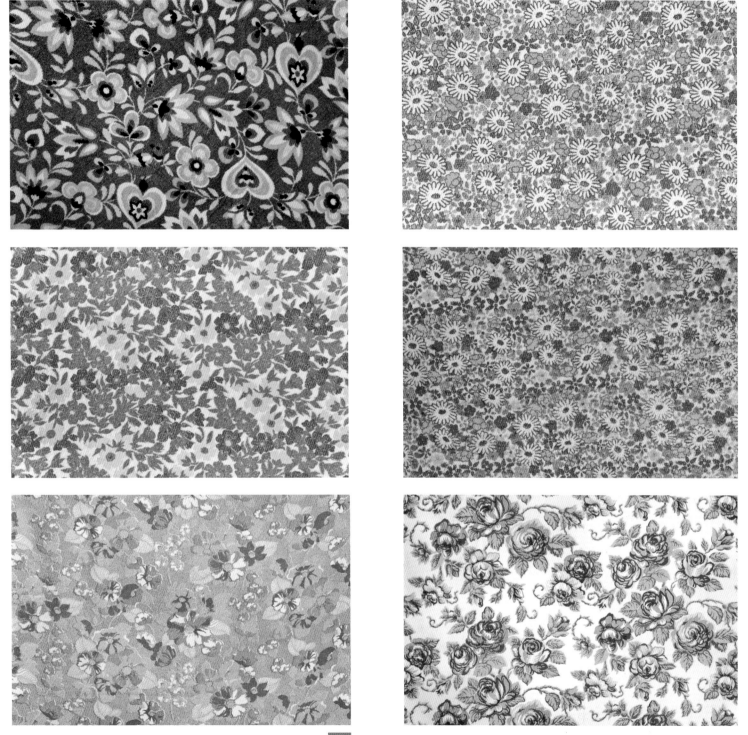

Florals–Traditional

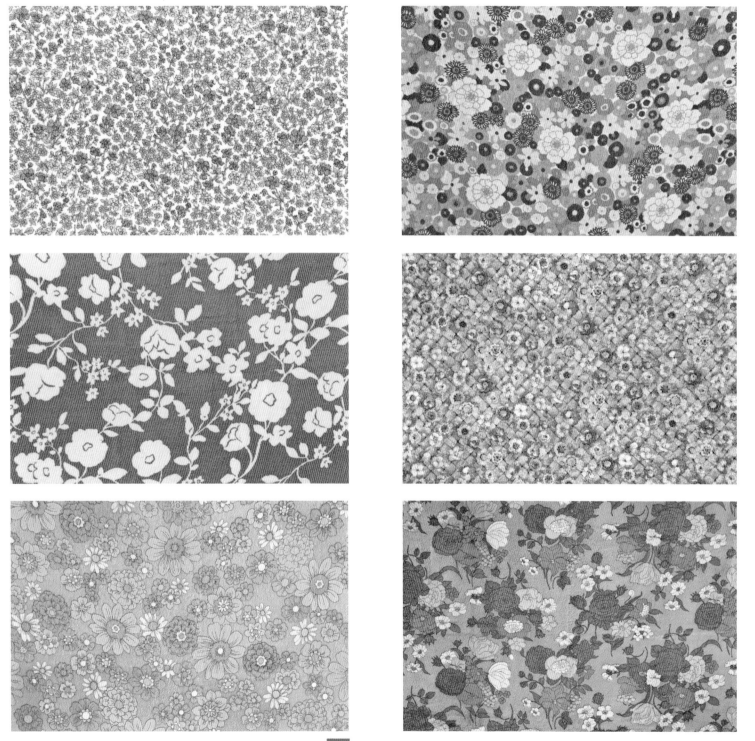

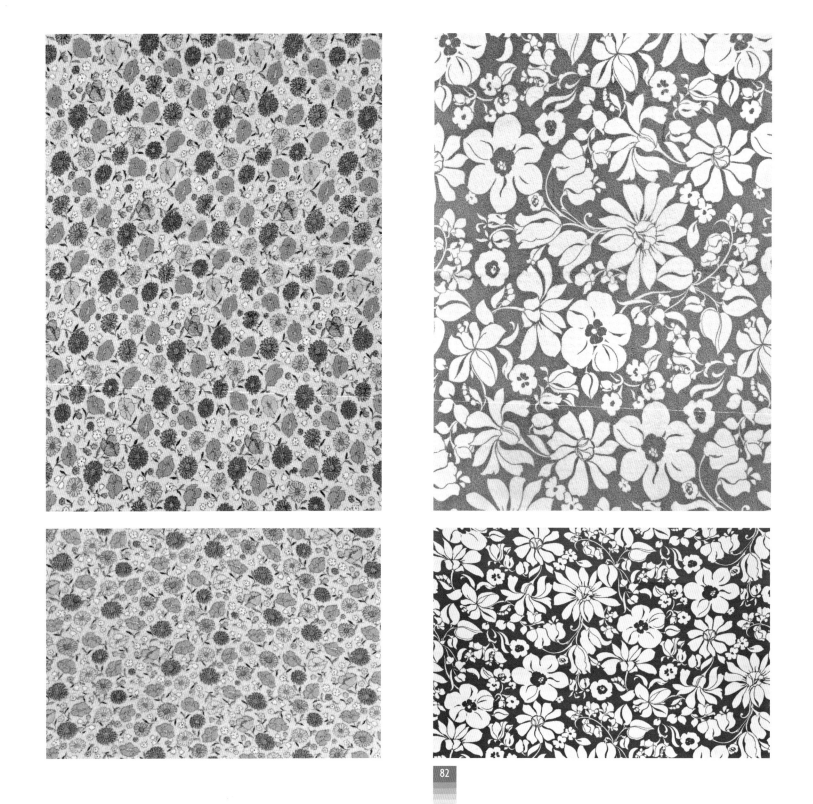

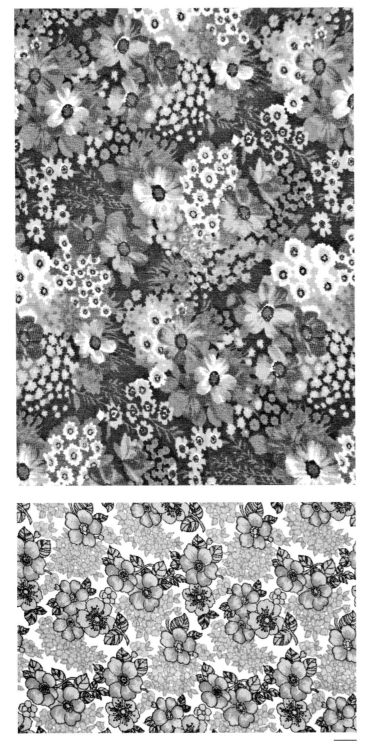

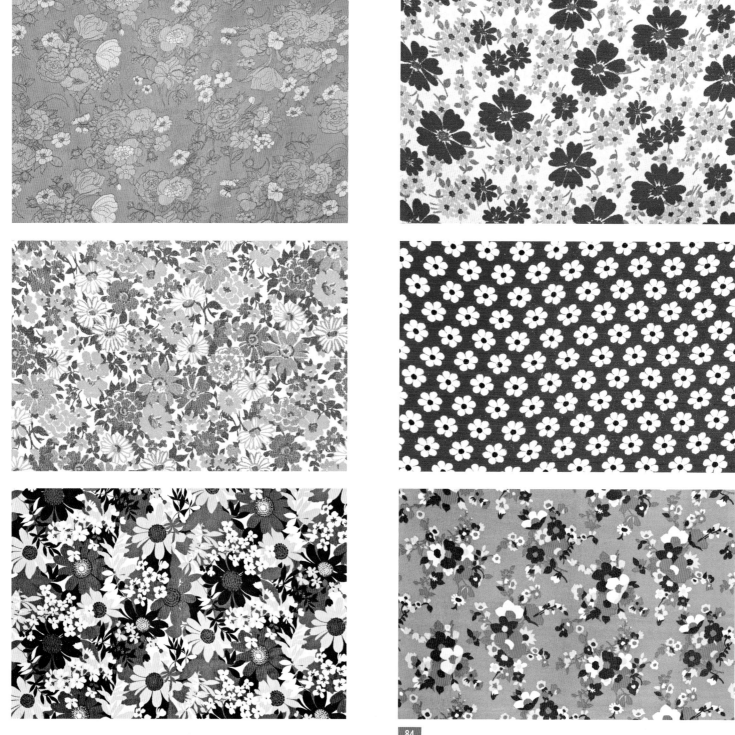

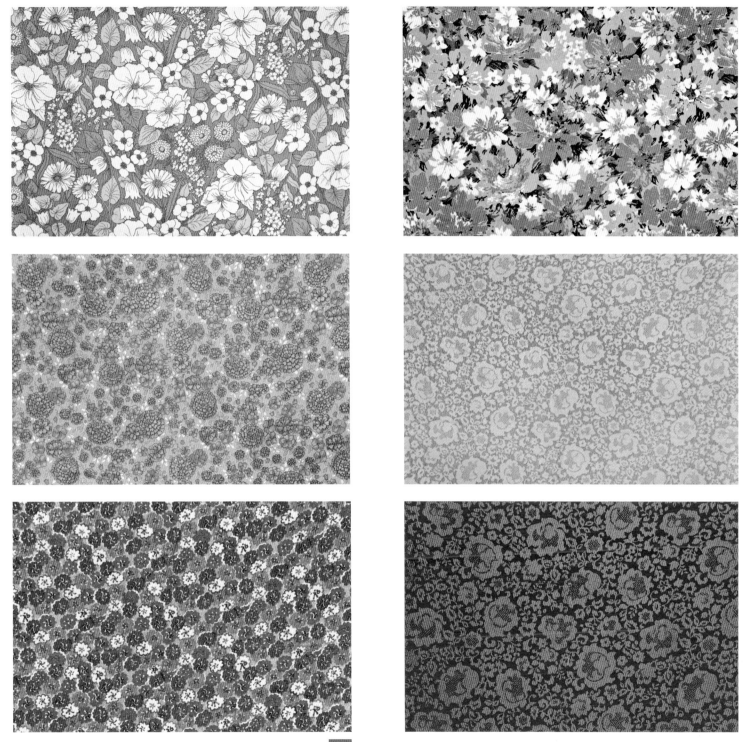

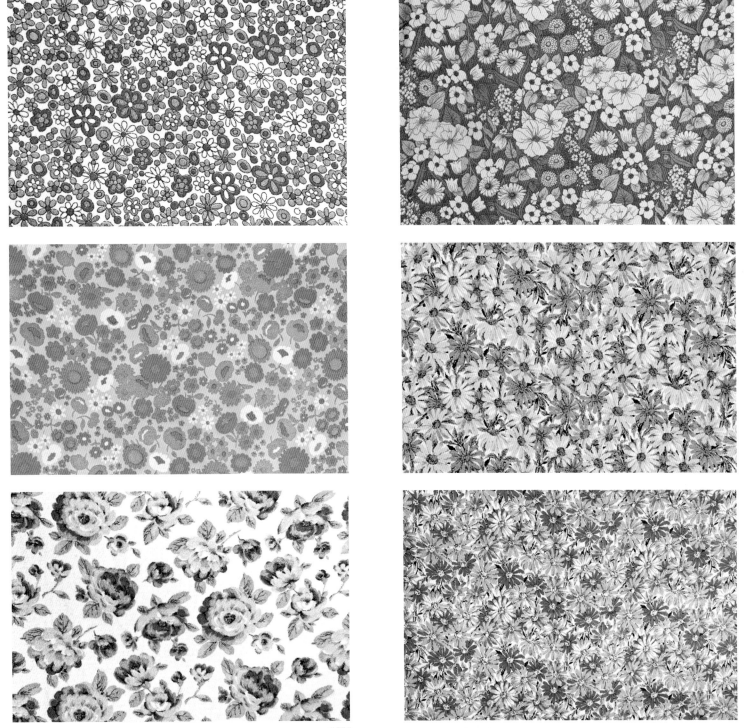

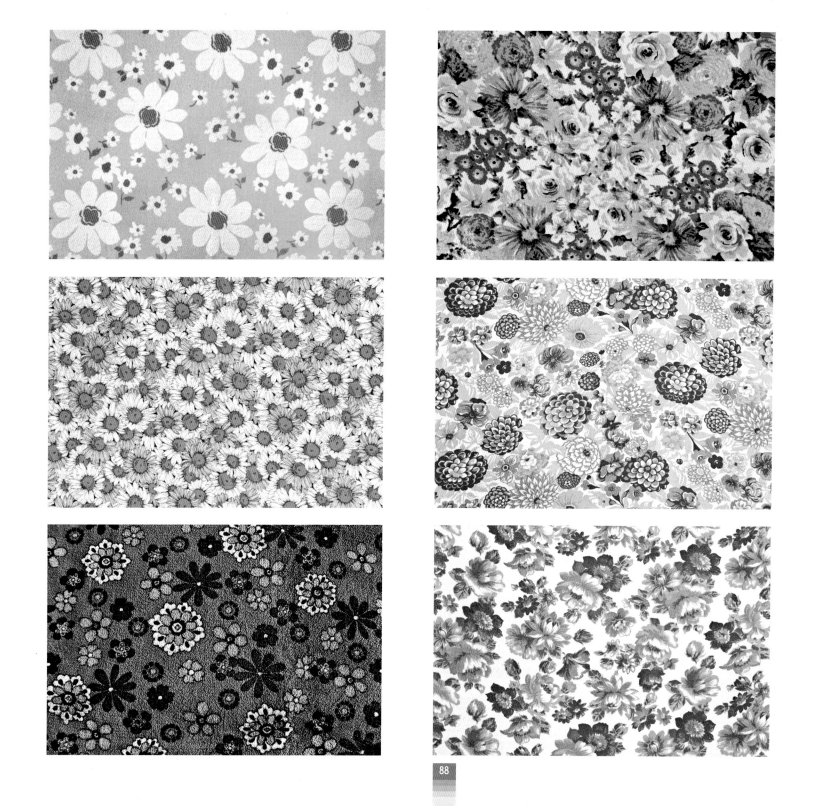

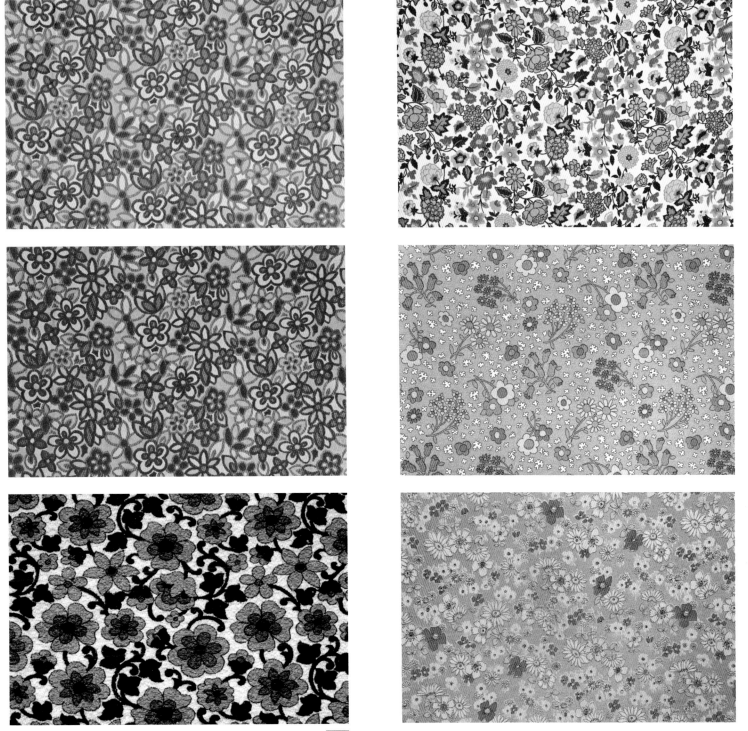

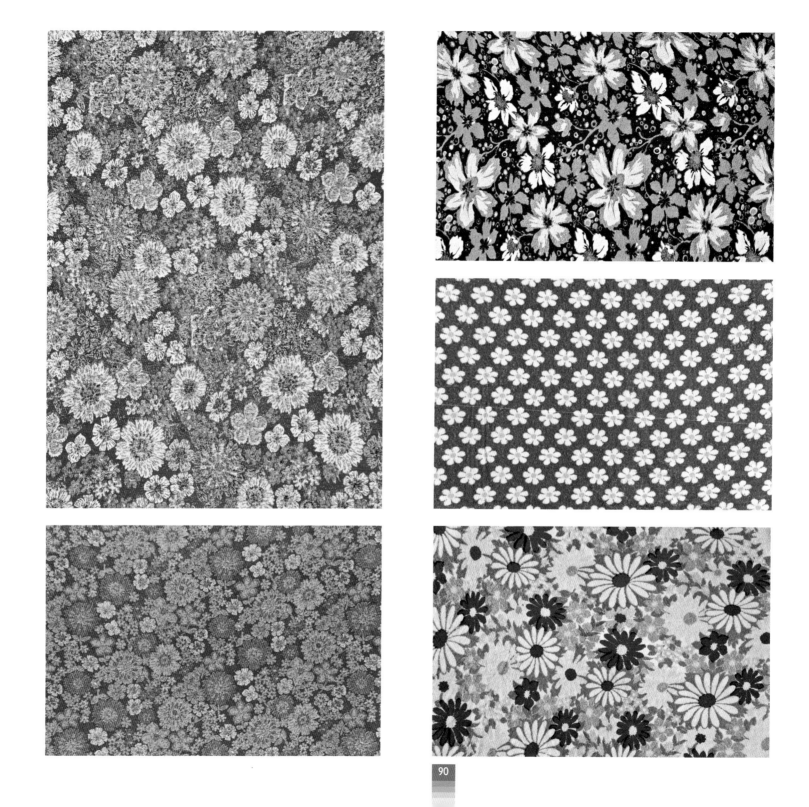

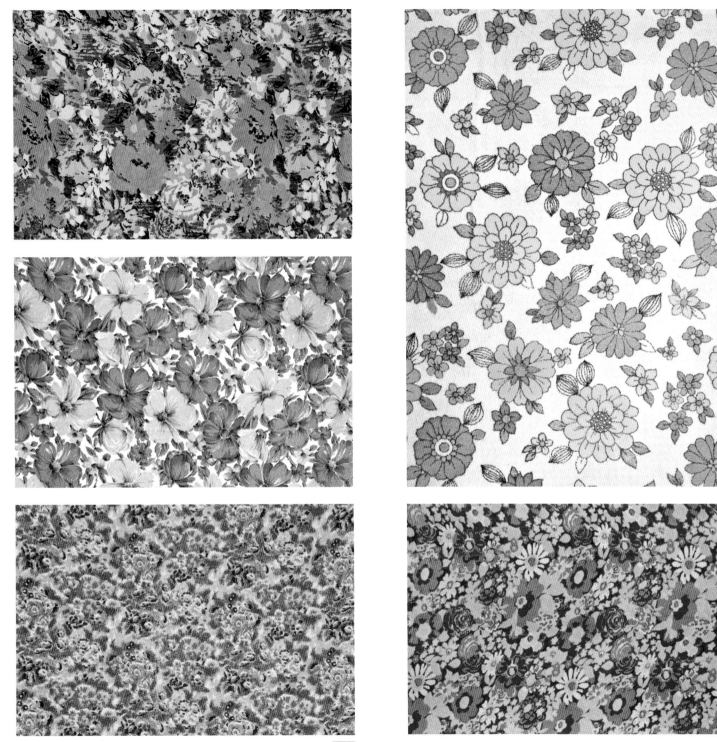

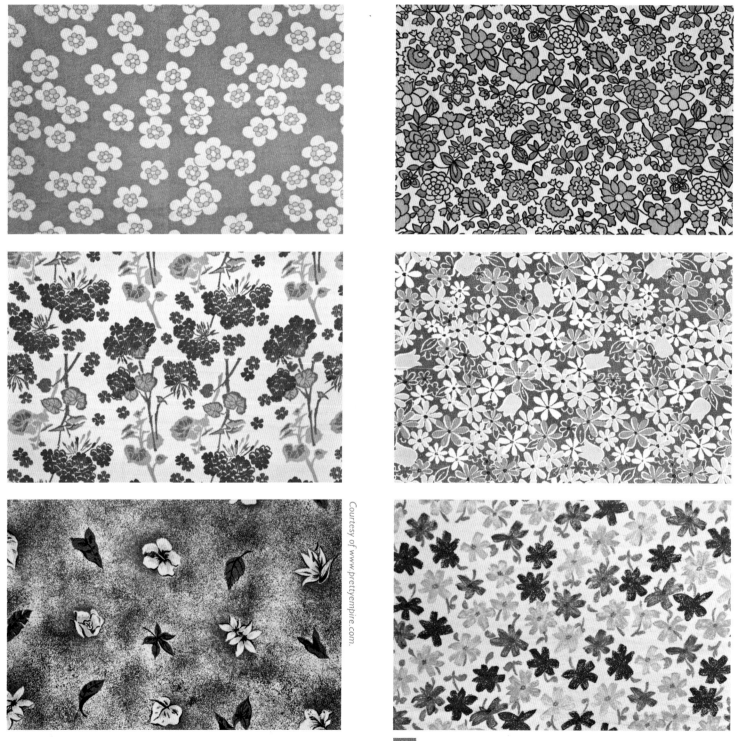

Courtesy of www.prettyempire.com.

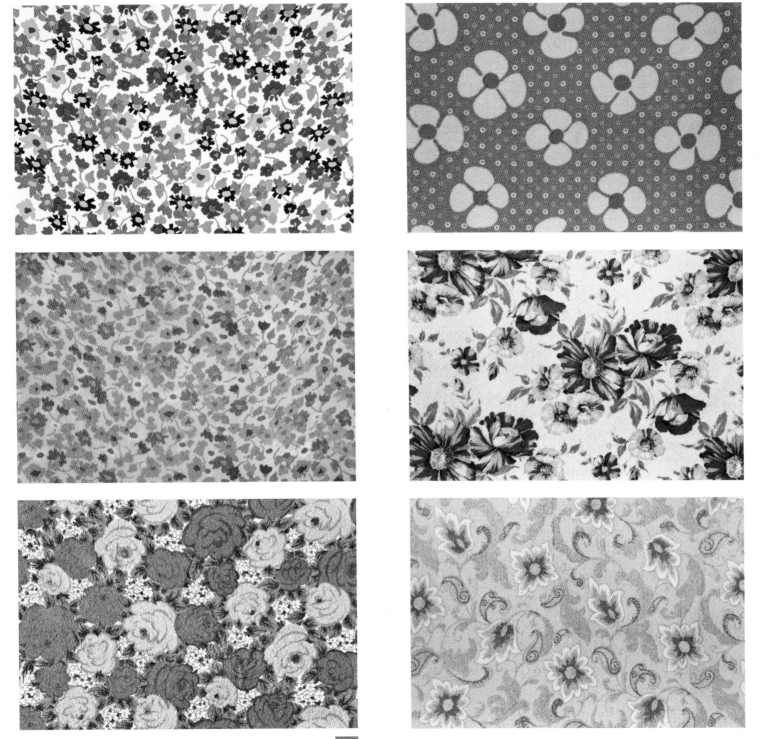

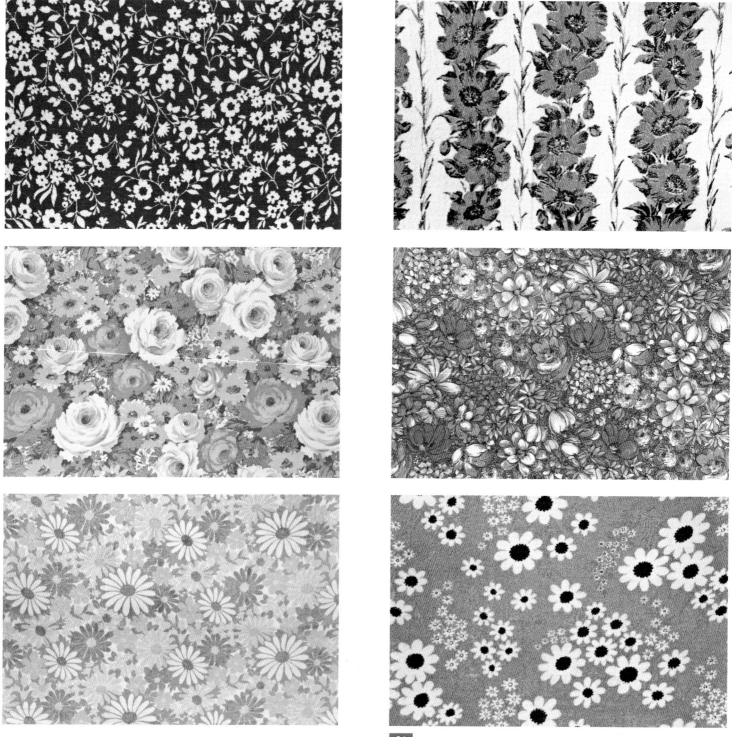

Florals–Traditional

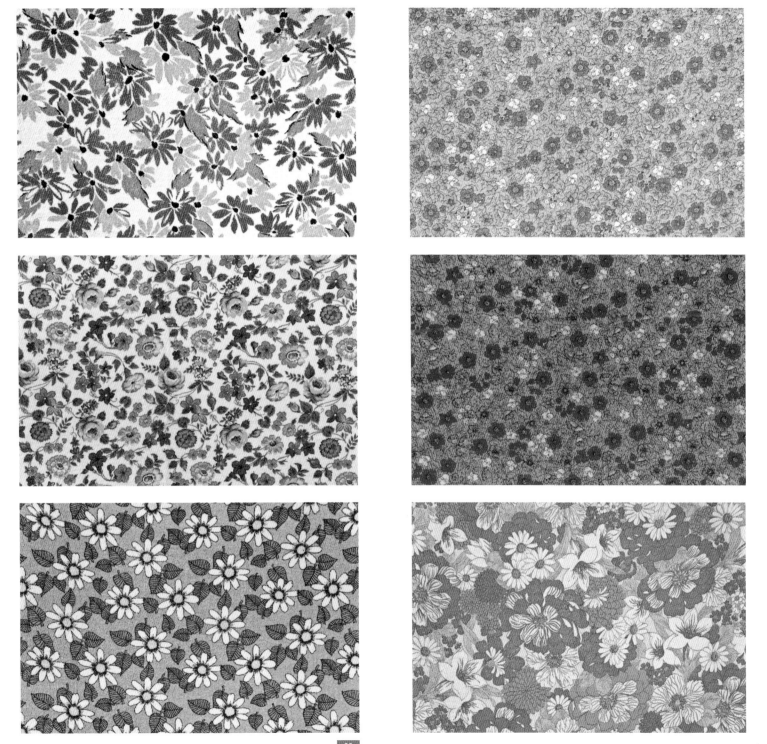

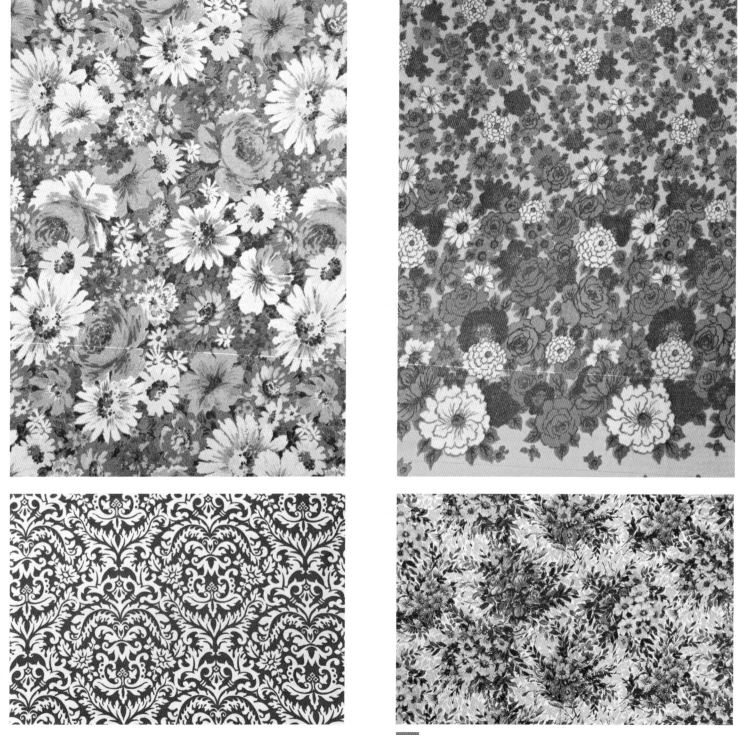

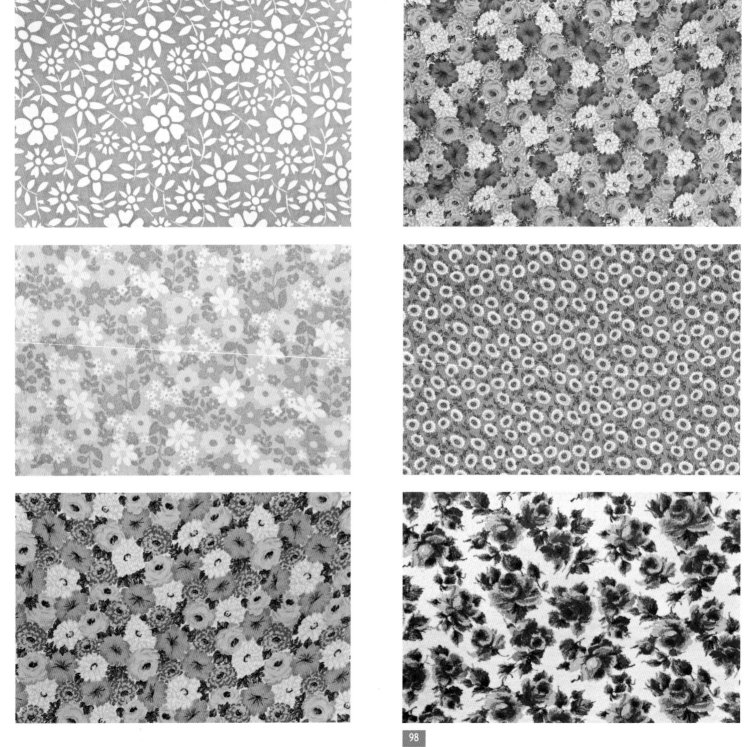

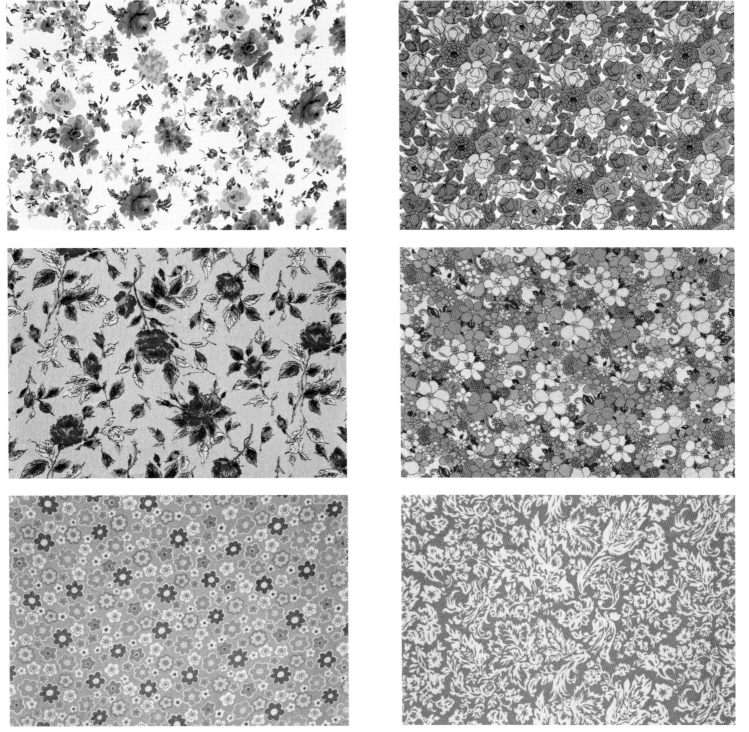

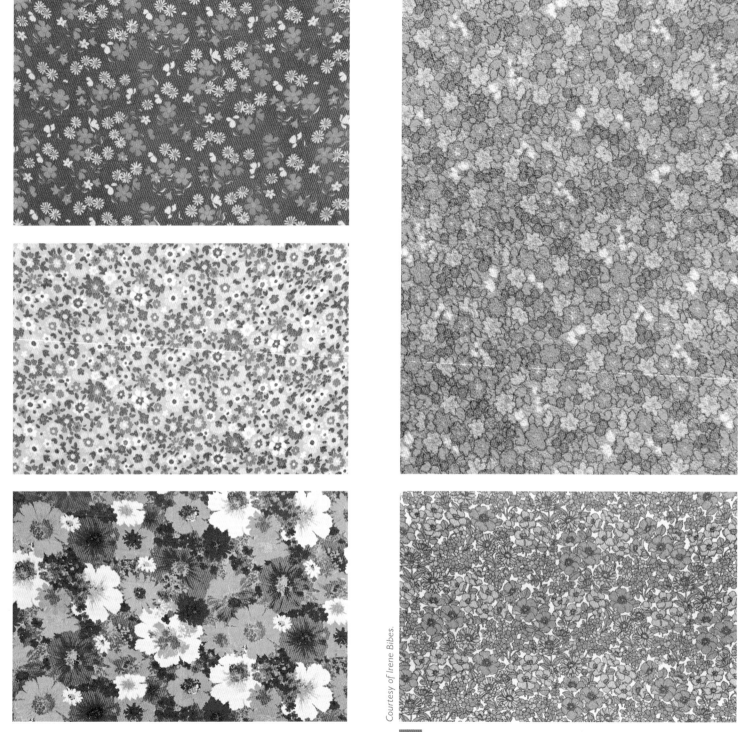

Courtesy of Irene Bibes.

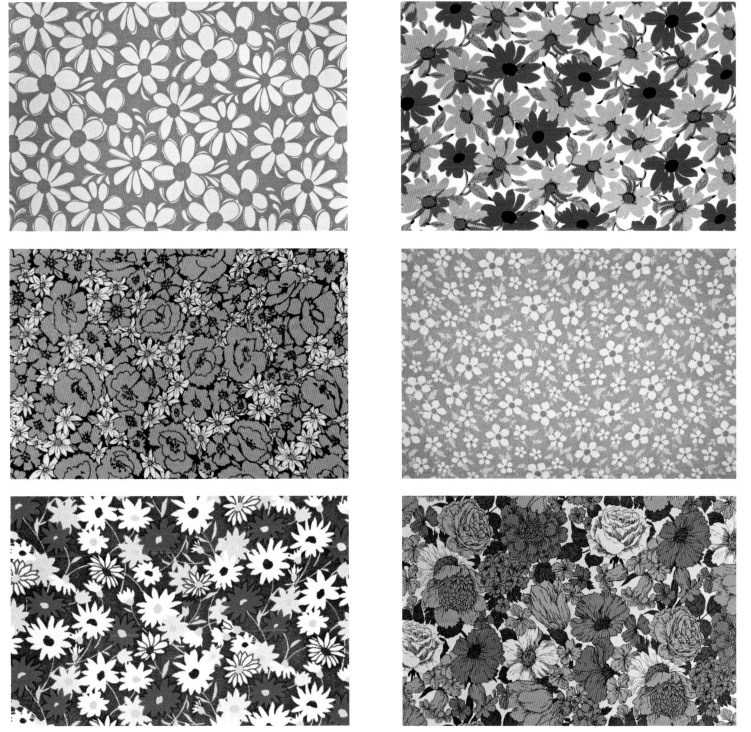

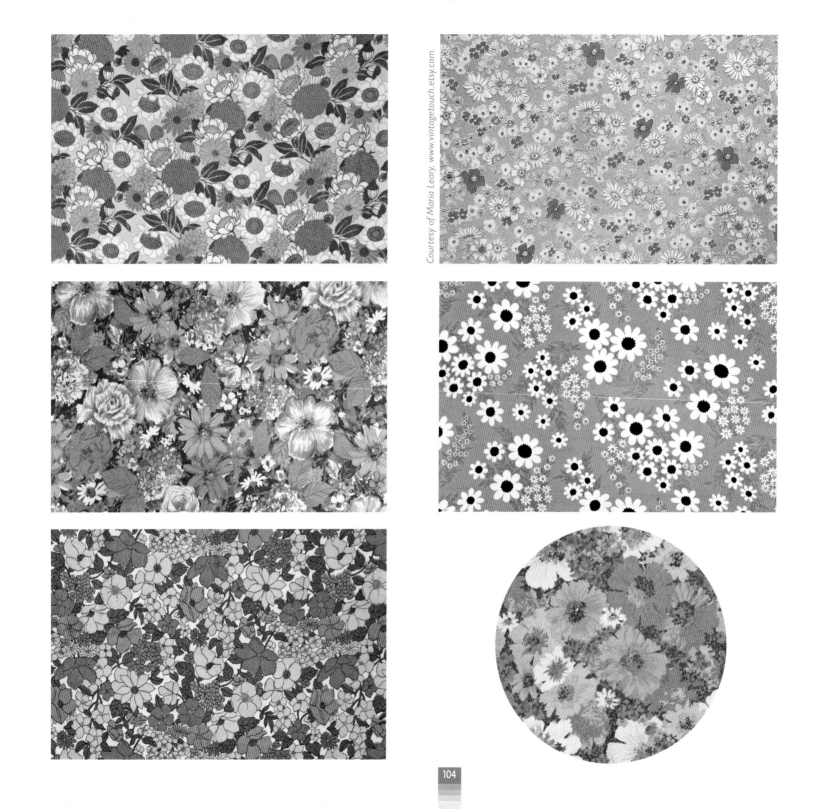

Courtesy of Maria Leary, www.vintagetouch.etsy.com.

Courtesy of Vanessa Jennings, www.vintagefabrics.com.au.

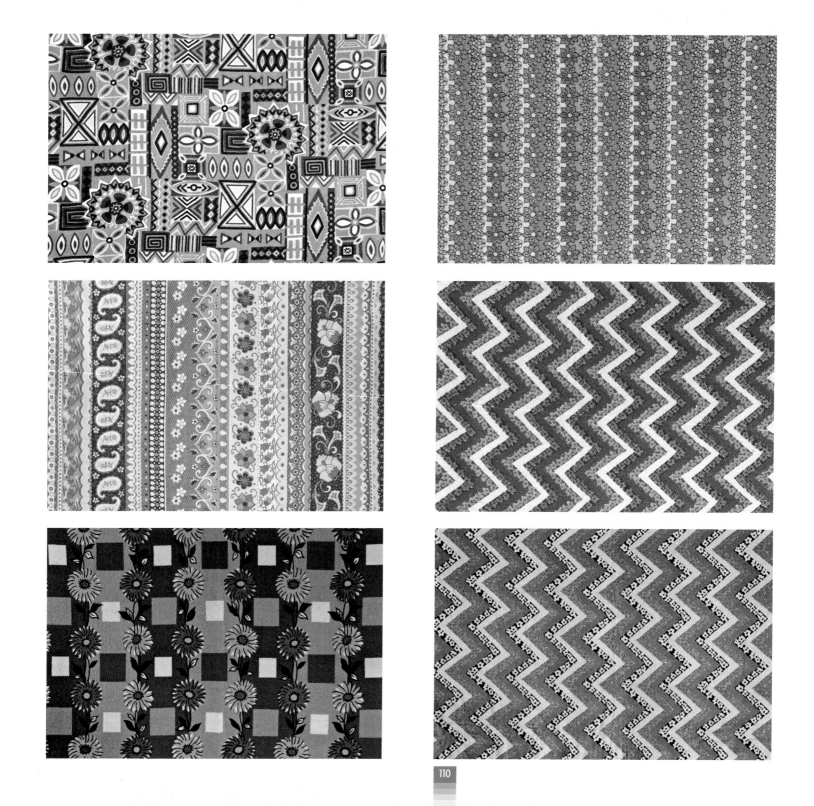

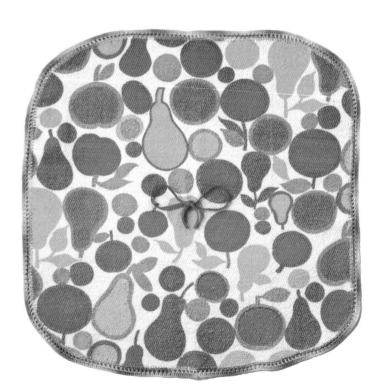

Fruits & Vegetables

114

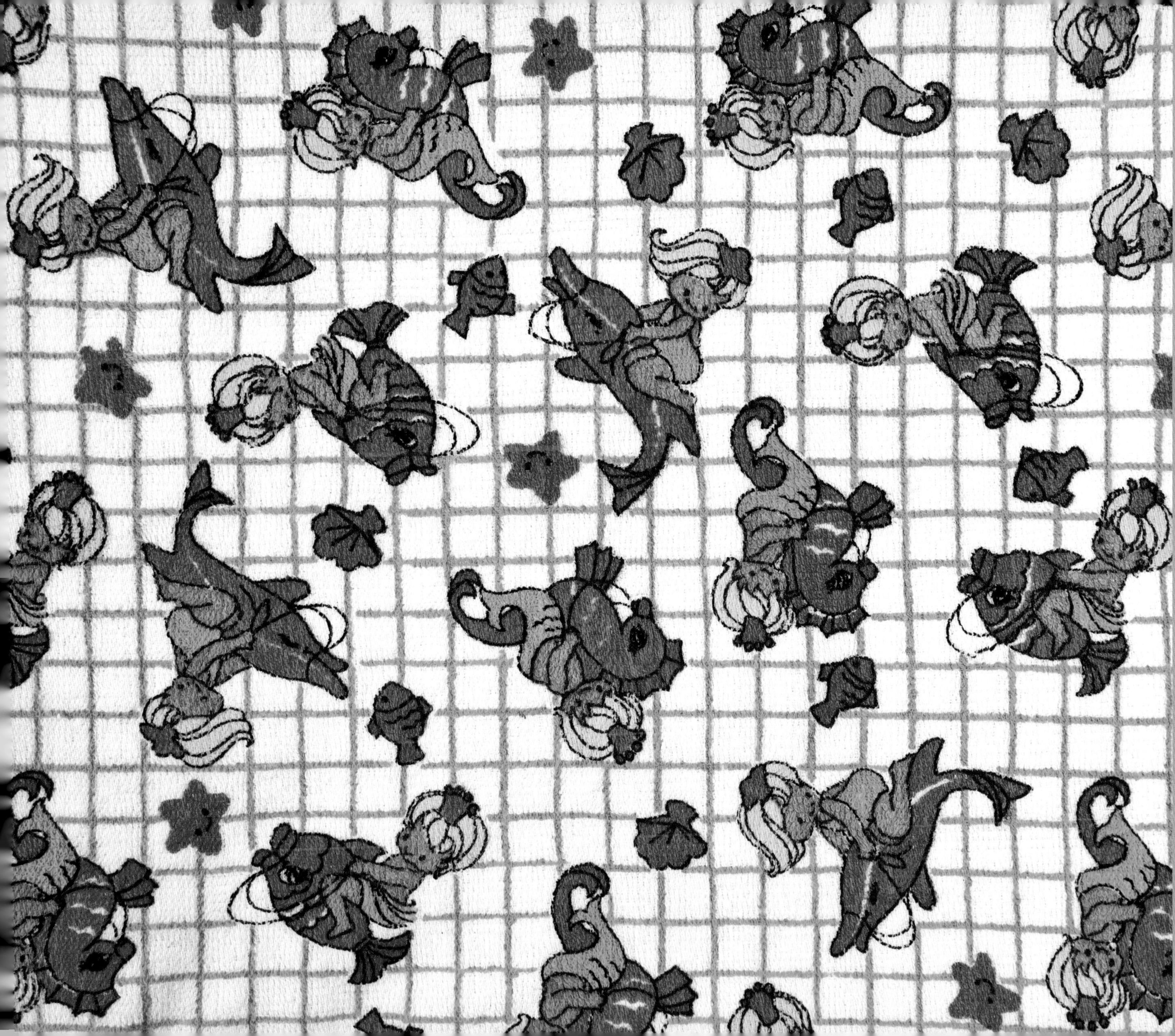

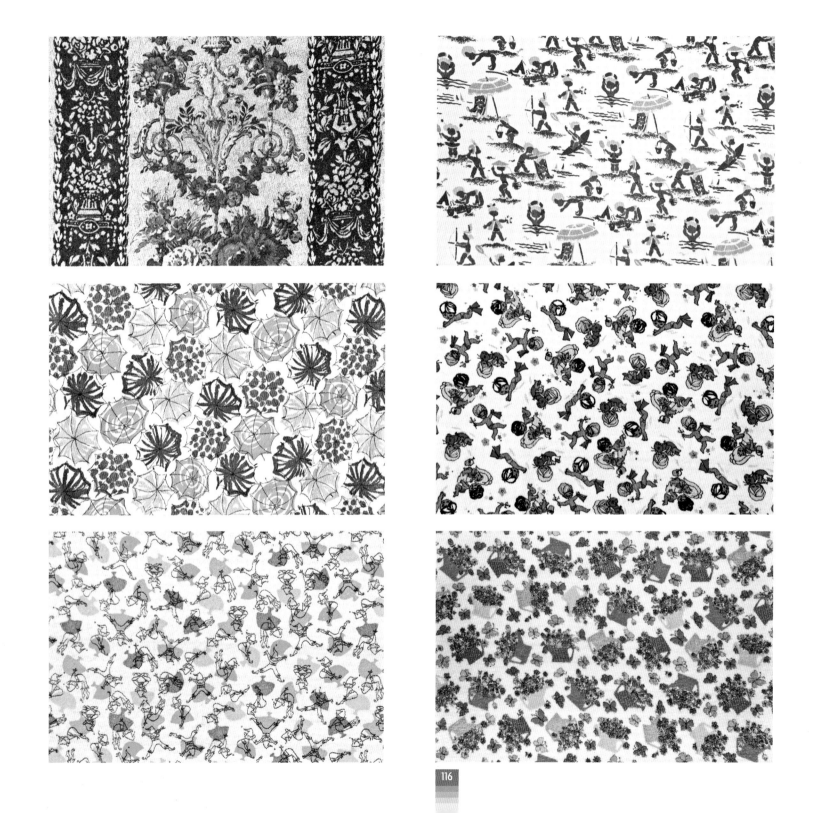

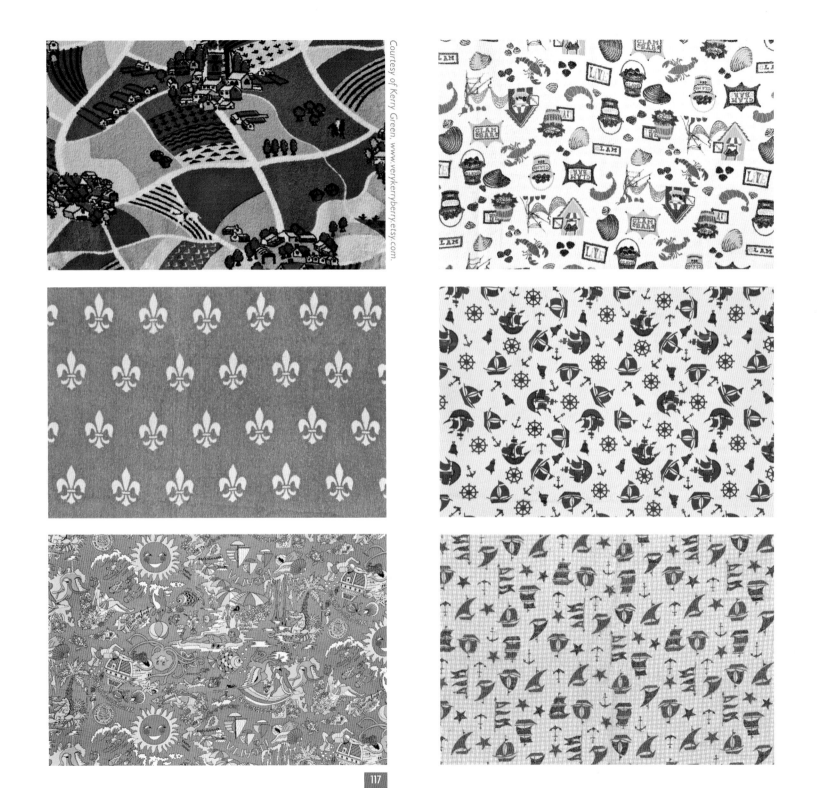

Courtesy of Cynthia Bond, www.pumpkintruck.etsy.com.

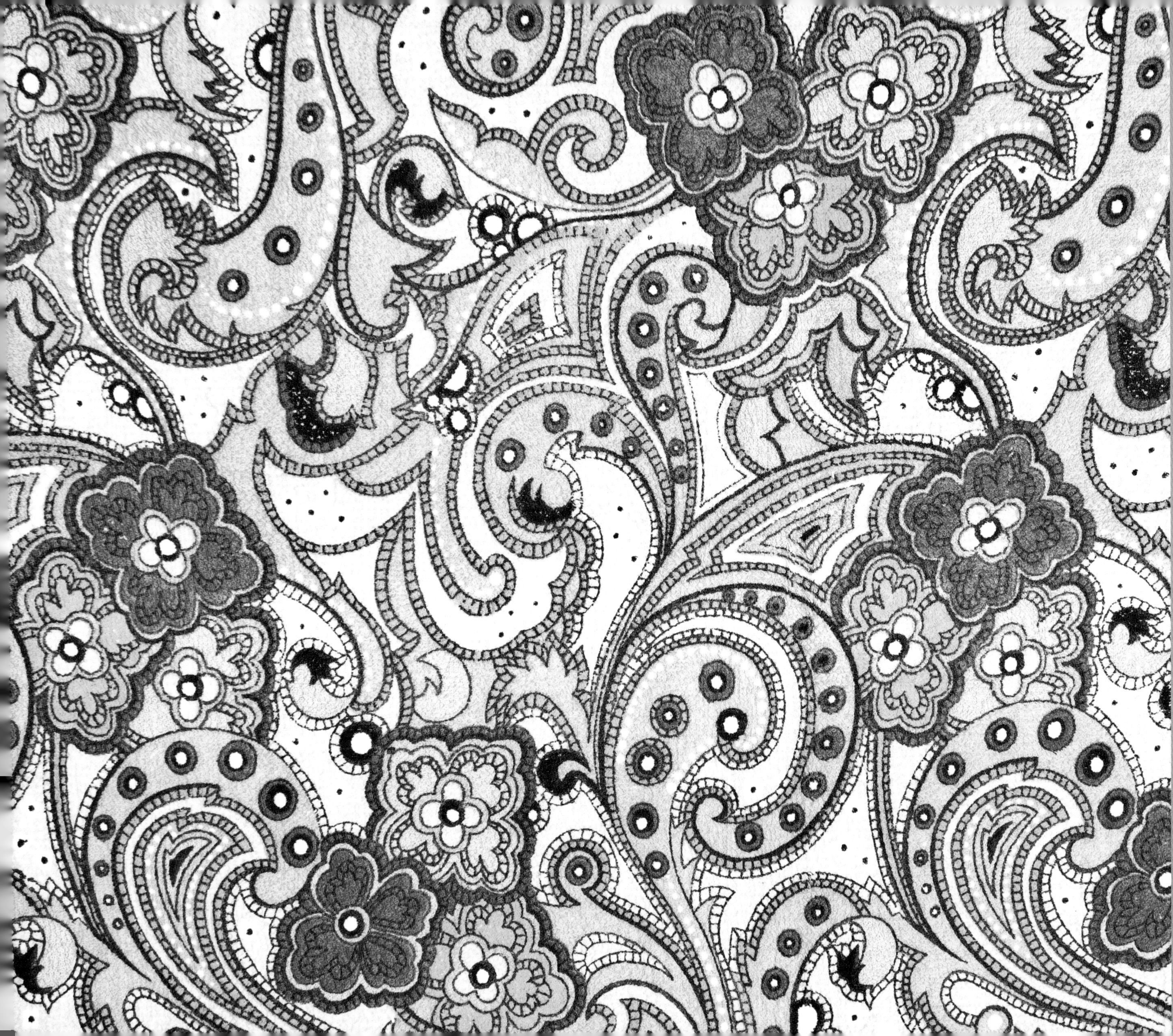

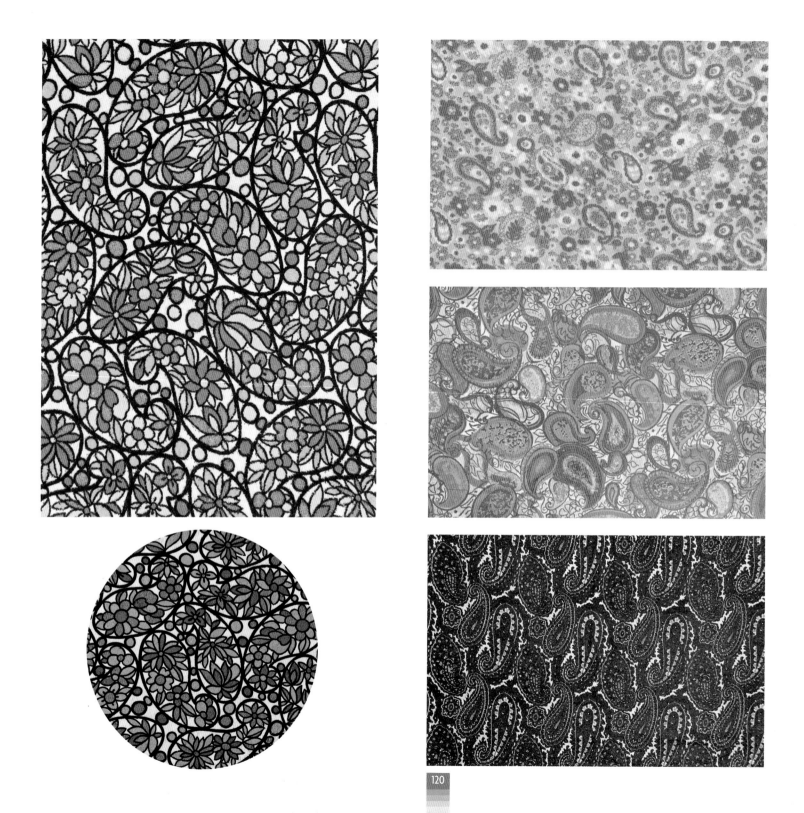

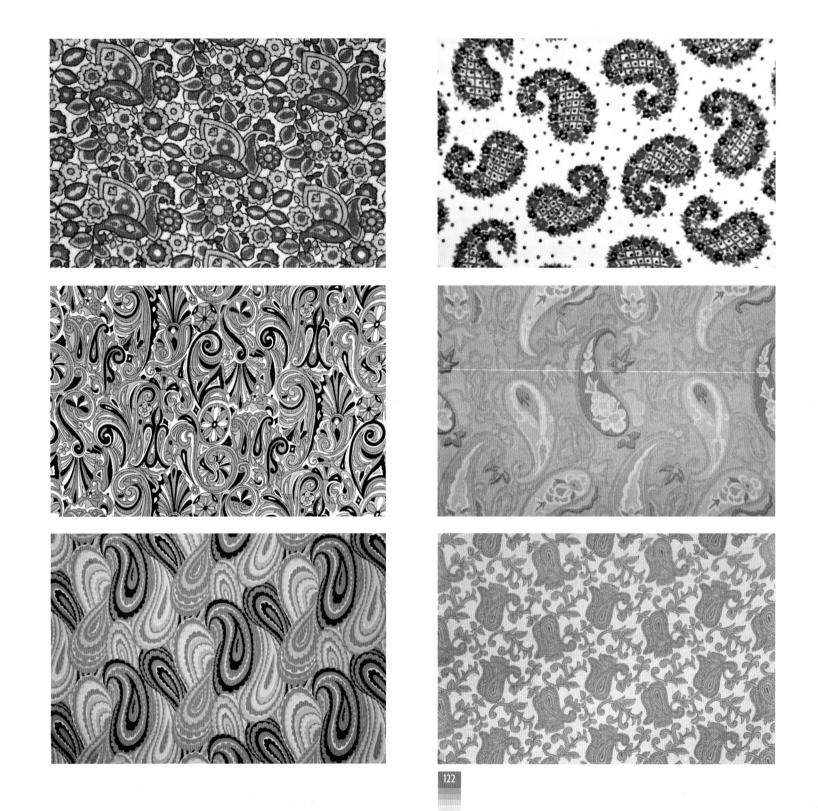

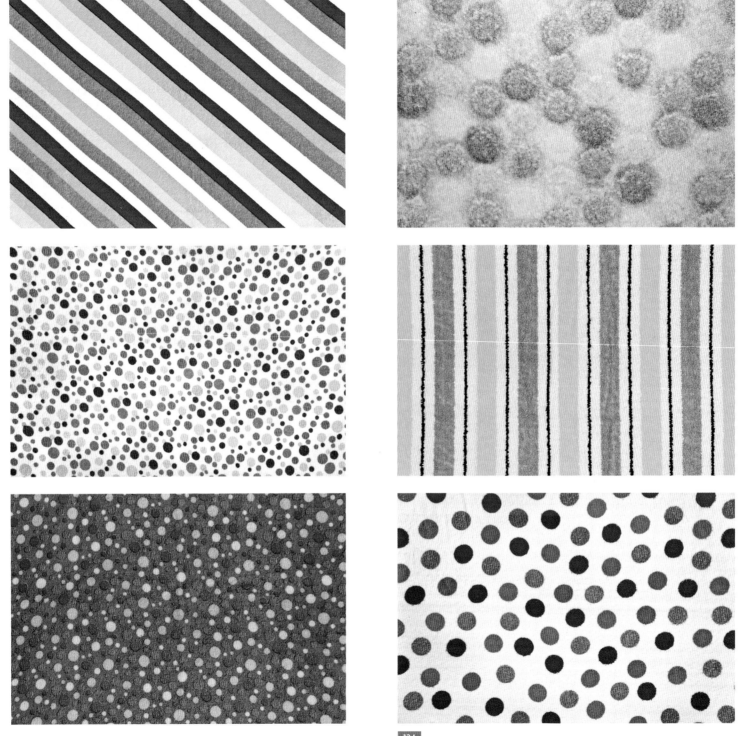

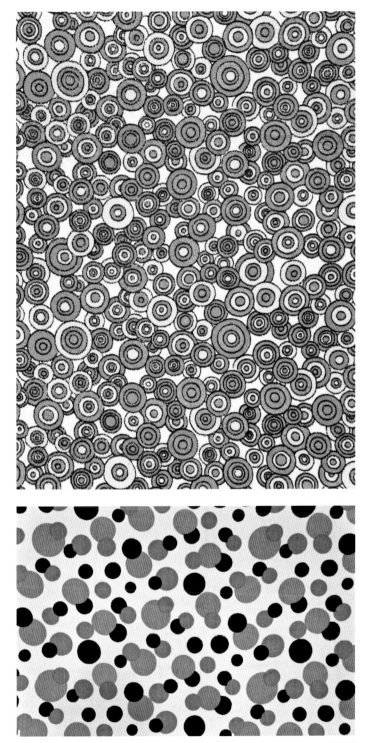
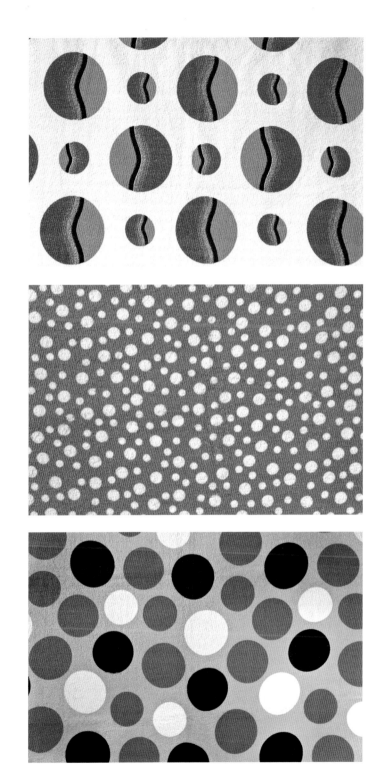

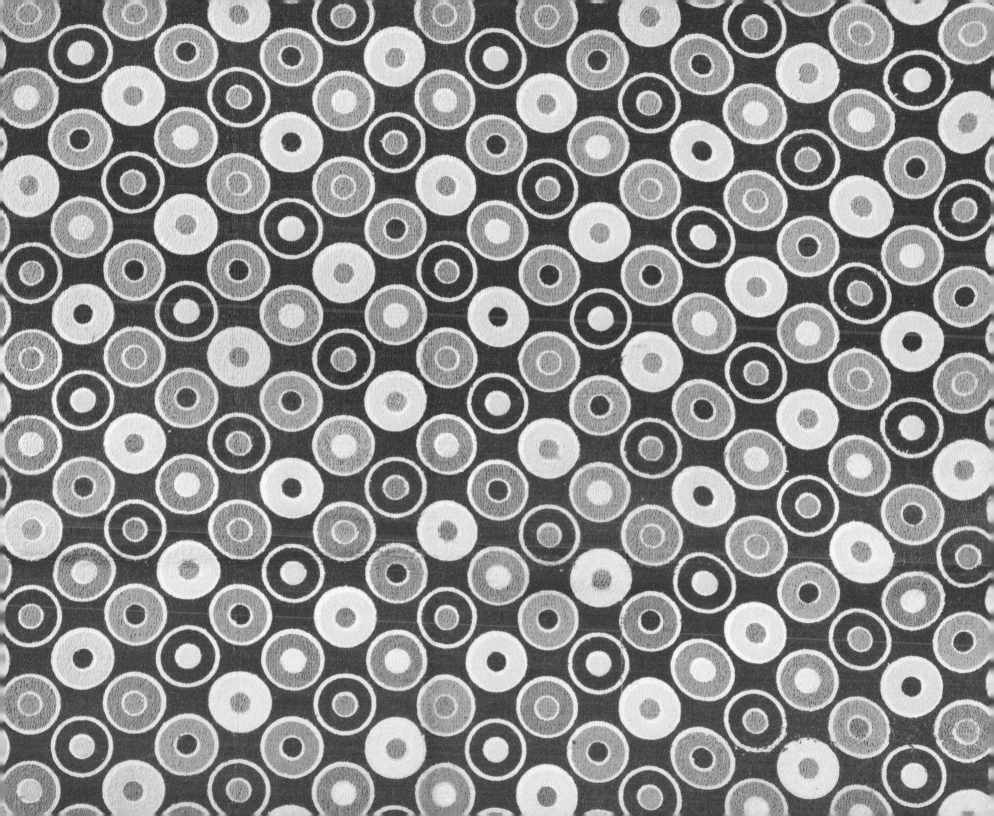

Endnotes

[1] *The Story of Cotton,* PDF online book published by www.cottoncounts.net, date unknown, p. 7.

[2] *Textiles and The Origin of Their Names* by Robert H. Megraw, published c.1906, p. 48.

[3] *Scissors and Yardstick* or *All About Dry Goods* by C. M. Brown and C. L. Gates, published 1872, p. 70.

[4] *A History of Industrial Paterson: Being a Compendium of the Establishment, Growth and Present Status in Paterson, NJ, of the Silk, Cotton, Flax, Locomotive, Iron and Miscellaneous Industries* by L. R. Trumbull, published 1882, p. 67.

[5] "An Early Impression of What Costume Designers Will Soon Be Offering for Spring Wear," *New York Times,* December 1911.

[6] *Dictionary of Dry Goods and A History of Silk, Cotton, Linen, Wool and other Fibrous Substances,* by George S. Cole, published 1894, p. 351.

[7] "Terry Cloth Varied in Summer Attire," *New York Times,* May 1949.

[8] "Terry Cloth Used for Beach Wear," *New York Times,* January 1950.

[9] "Toweling Turns to Brighter Hues," *New York Times,* August 1956.

[10] "Nightgowns Show Up at Best Parties," *Schenectady Gazette,* January 1971.

[11] "Suddenly Terry Cloth Big in Today's Fashions," *Sarasota Journal,* February 1977.

[12] "Terry Cloth: All Dressed Up," *New York Times,* April 1979.

[13] "Color returns to male clothes," *Calgary Herald,* January 1979.

Resources

Fabric Sources
www.americanterry.com
www.ebay.com
www.etsy.com
www.fabric.com
www.fashionfabricsonline.com
www.joanns.com
www.superbuzzy.com
www.tactilethreads.com
www.vintagefabricaddict.com
www.vintagefabrics.com.au

History/Technical Information
www.wearinghistoryblog.com
www.coutureallure.blogspot.com
www.thepeoplehistory.com
www.cottoninc.com
www.athm.org (American Textile History Museum)
www.textilehistory.org
www.home.iprimus.com.au/metzke/references2.html (Historical Weaving Mills)
www.nationaltextile.org
www.colorantshistory.org
www.textileheritagemuseum.org
www.pratthistory.com
www.cottonmuseum.com
www.cotton.org
www.spinningtheweb.org.uk
www.textilemuseum.org
www.teonline.com
www.kipnotes.com/textiles
www.hctar.org (Harvard Center for Textile & Apparel Research)
www.trueup.net
www.prettyempire.com

Books for Further Reading
The Buying and Care of Towels and Sheets. New York, New York: Cannon Mills Inc., circa 1940s.

Love and a Few Stitches. New York, New York: Cannon Mills Inc., 1972.

Yafa, Stephen. *Cotton: The Biography of a Revolutionary Fiber.* New York, New York: Penguin Books, 2005.